Inspiration™

FOR GREEKS

ENCOURAGEMENT

HUMOR & MOTIVATION

FOR

GREEKS

BY

GREEKS

The Collegiate
EmPowerment Company, Inc.
www.Collegiate-EmPowerment.com
Toll Free: 1.877.338.8246

**The
Collegiate
EmPowerment
Company, Inc.**

"The Leader in EmPowerment Education for Tod___"

Co Authored By: ANTONY J. D'ANGELO,
RICK BARNES, DAMIEN DUCHAMP,
LISA FEDLER, MONICA LEE MIRANDA,
RICK MORAT, & BETH SAUL

Published by:

The Collegiate EmPowerment Company, Inc.

"The Leader in EmPowerment Education for Today's College Students"

PO BOX 702 LAMBERTVILLE, NEW JERSEY 08530
WWW.COLLEGIATE-EMPOWERMENT.COM
Toll Free: 1-877-EDUTAIN (338.8246)

Printed with Pride in The United States Of America
ISBN: 0-9646957-2-3

BOOKS ARE AVAILABLE IN QUANTITY DISCOUNTS WHEN USED FOR GREEK RECRUITMENT, DEVELOPMENT, TRAINING OR RECOGNITION. FOR PRICING INFORMATION PLEASE SEE PAGE 140 AT THE BACK OF THIS BOOK. THANK YOU.

Supporting The People Who Support Greeks

In the spirit of empowering today's college students,
The Collegiate EmPowerment Company, Inc.,recognizes
The Association of Fraternity Advisors (AFA)
as the Charitable Benefactor of Inspiration for Greeks.
The Collegiate EmPowerment Company, will donate
One Dollar from every book sold to AFA.
This money will help support AFA
as it pursues its Mission & Vision.

The AFA Mission:

As the representative voice of and advocate for our profession, the Association of Fraternity Advisors exists to support the professional development of our members, foster partnerships across higher education, and offer innovative resources and services to persons involved in the advancement of fraternities and sororities.

The AFA Vision:

The Association of Fraternity Advisors will be the essential professional association for men and women involved in the fraternity/sorority movement. The core values of education, collaboration, professionalism, inclusivity, integrity and honesty will guide our decision making and our actions. We will focus on advancing the fraternity/sorority advising profession, the professional development of our members, expanding programs and services, increasing and broadening our membership, streamlining our operations, and strengthening existing and forging new relationships which impact the Association.

Association of Fraternity Advisors, Inc.
3901 West 86th Street, Suite 165
Indianapolis, IN 46268
PHONE: 317.876.1632 FAX: 317.876.3981
www.fraternityadvisors.org

The Inspiration Book Series

TABLE OF CONTENTS

Welcome To The Inspiration Book Series!

Dear Friend,

Thank you for reading Inspiration for Greeks. The book you are holding has been made possible by people just like you.

This book, as well as the entire The Inspiration Book Series, is a compilation of stories of encouragement, humor & motivation by college students for college students. This book is for YOU and by YOU.

This whole "Inspiration Revolution" was started by two college students just like you, Dan Oltersdorf & Amy Connolly, the co-authors of Inspiration for Resident Assistants. The vision which we had back in 1999 has now manifested itself into a seven part book series. This book is number two in the series.

From the outset, our vision was never to create a New York Times Bestseller. Rather it has been our vision to create of vehicle for college students to inspire each other with their own story.

Research shows us that 80% of all college students join a student organization, like a fraternity or sorority, for one fundamental reason: To make a friend. A connection with the world around them.

The word Inspiration means "In Spirit". As fraternity men and sorority women, we don't just join our chapters because of the way we look or because of the clothes we wear. No, there is more to being Greek than this.

Being Greek is a spirit, something that transcends the things around us. It is a spirit that not only comes from us, but it is also a spirit that comes through us. It unites us and gives a common bond worldwide.

We need this bond now more than ever. You see the sad reality is that most people are not getting what they want. Not from their education, not from their jobs, not from their families, not from their religion, not from their government, not from one another and most importantly, not from themselves. Something is missing in most of our lives.

What most people need is a place of community that has higher purpose and deeper meaning. A place in which being human is a prerequisite, but acting human is essential. A place that replaces the home that many of us have seemingly lost.

That is what your fraternity or sorority can be. It can become the place of community. It can become a place where words such as integrity, concern, compassion, vision and excellence can be used not as nouns, but as action verbs. The kind of place that gives people a sense that your chapter is a special place, created by special people doing what they do in the best possible way. And all being done for the simplest, most human reason possible- because they are alive! What other reason do we need?

Human beings are capable of performing extraordinary acts. Capable of going to the moon. Capable of bottling powdered tea mix and then selling it for 100 times the cost of making it. Capable of building computers. Capable of creating killer equations like $e=mc^2$. Capable of making Tupperware lids that fit. Capable of flying planes filled with people into our national treasures.

The least we should be able to do is create a sense of community on our campus. A sense of caring. Caring for our school. Caring for our chapters. Caring for ourselves and most of all, caring for one another.

As Richard Bach writes in the book, Jonathan Livingston Seagull. "The bond that links your true family is not one of blood, but the respect and joy in each other's life. Rarely do members of one family grow up under the same roof."

Even though we may have never met before in person, we have all met in spirit. The spirit of Brotherhood & Sisterhood.

In The Spirit which bonds us all,
Anthony J. D'Angelo
The Creator of The Inspiration Book Series ™

About The Authors:

Anthony J. D'Angelo, The Collegiate EmPowerment Coach™, is a brother of **Theta Chi Fraternity** and a graduate of West Chester University of PA. He is the founder of **The Collegiate EmPowerment Company** (CEC) and the creator of The Inspiration Book Series™. Since 1995 Tony and The CEC Team have served over 1 Million college students from over 1,000 schools across North America, Europe & Australia.

Rick Barnes has been involved professionally with fraternity & sorority life for more than 17 years. He currently works at **Texas Christian University** as the Director of Special Projects for Student Affairs. Rick is a past president of the Association of Fraternity Advisors and a member of **FarmHouse Fraternity**. In addition he has been a featured speaker on more than 100 college campuses.

Damien Duchamp is the Assistant Director of Student Life Programs at **Indiana State University** and the Assistant Executive Director of the National Pan-Hellenic Council, Inc. Damien is a member of two Greek organizations, Sigma Beta Chi Fraternity (local) and **Phi Beta Sigma Fraternity, Inc.** He is an active alumnus of both groups, and has served on the national board for Phi Beta Sigma. Damien received a B.A. in Communication Media from SUNY New Paltz and an M.Ed. in Counseling and Educational Leadership from Clemson University. He is active in the AFA and is currently pursuing a Ph.D. in Higher Education and Student Affairs at Indiana University.

Lisa Fedler is the Director of Member Services for the **North-American Interfraternity Conference** (NIC) and has worked at Bowling Green State University and Southern Missouri State University. Lisa is a member of **Sigma Kappa Sorority** and currently serves Sigma Kappa as the Director of Member Development. In addition, she has been recognized for her contributions to the profession as a recipient of the Beta Theta Pi Interfraternalism Award, The AFA Perspectives Award, NASPA's Rising Star Award and the creation of the Lisa L. Fedler Greek Humanitarian and Unity Award at Bowling Green State University.

Monica Lee Miranda currently serves as Director of Greek Affairs at the **University of Rochester**. As an undergraduate at the University at Albany she joined the Alpha Chapter of **Omega Phi Beta Sorority, Inc.** and has been a proud and active member for the past 8 years. A volunteer for the AFA, Monica was awarded their 2000 Diversity Initiative Award. As a recognized leader in the Latino Greek movement she has served as Vice chair for the National Association of Latino Fraternal Organizations, Inc. (NALFO) and was honored with the first Rising Professional Award at the Annual National Latino Greek Awards. In addition Monica has published several articles and presents nationally on a variety of topics. She is currently pursuing a PhD in Higher Education at the University of Rochester.

Rick Morat is the Director of Student Activities and University Center at **University of the Pacific** in Stockton, California. He is a former president of the Association of Fraternity Advisors (AFA) and the AFA Foundation. He has twice received the AFA distinguished Service award. Rick currently chairs the Interfraternal Task Force on Alcohol-Free Fraternity Housing. Rick became a member of **Sigma Chi Fraternity** at Central Michigan University.

Beth Saul is the Associate Director for Greek Life at the **University of Southern California** and the Executive Director for Gamma Sigma Alpha National Greek Academic Honor Society. She is a member of **Alpha Epsilon Phi**, served as the NPC Chairman and NPC Academic Excellence Chair, and is currently on the NPC College Panhellenics Committee and Chairman of the NPC Centennial. She has received awards and honors from the NIC, AFA, NIF, the University of Southern California, Zeta Beta Tau, and Kappa Delta. She has been a facilitator at both UIFI and LeaderShape.

Acknowledgements:

This project would not be possible without the support, guidance & Inspiration of the following individuals:

Pamela Moss, the world most supportive assistant & associate editor. Pam you are a treasure to us all.

Taralynn Ross, of Browndog Design, the Goddess of Graphic Design. TL you bring life to the Vision.

Kay Hayes, of The PerfectWord. Thank you for transforming over 200 submissions into this book.

Sue Kraft, of the Association of Fraternity Advisors. Thanks for your Faith in us. Here's to our partnership!

Charlie Warner, a Mentor & Past-President of AFA. Thanks for helping us to create a solid team.

TJ Sullivan, of Campuspeak, Inc.. Thanks for your suggestions & recommendations.

Dave Westol, Executive Director of Theta Chi Fraternity Thanks for your guidance & direction.

To our families, friends and colleagues who gave us the love & support we needed to make this book a reality.

And most of all to the Spirit of our Fraternity Brothers & Sorority Sisters who came before us. May you be with us all in this journey. Thank you for the legacy.

An Investment
by Rev. Will S. Keim, PhD

We live in a society where communication possibilities are so numerous it seems absurd that people could be living lives of quiet desperation. Yet this happens on every campus everywhere. I experienced this isolation and loneliness for three weeks in 1971 when I went to college and my assigned roommate never showed up. For three weeks I went to class alone, ate alone, and slept in a really quiet room in a freshman residence hall. I considered dropping out of school but then, at my darkest moment, four hundred miles away from home, a miraculous blessing took place.

Some guys on the baseball team who were in a fraternity knew I was going to go out for baseball and dropped by one Friday afternoon to ask me to come over for pizza and to play cards. With all my high school buddies a six-hour drive away in Los Angeles, I was thrilled to have some new friends. We sat around, played cards, ate pizza, with dessert provided by two of the fellows girlfriends that dropped by and had a great evening. It wasn't the dean of students, resident assistant, or a faculty person who had made me feel welcome for the first time. It was a group of men who would soon become my brothers.

People sometimes say, "You are Greek? I didn't have to buy my friends." I never get defensive. I say, "I did. I paid a two hundred dollar initiation fee in 1971 and since that time I have had over fifty thousand friends in Delta Upsilon. It was a pretty darn good investment." My new brothers came and watched me pitch, I in turn went and watched them play water polo or perform their music. We were brothers ... but not just then ... it continues to this day.

When my little brother decided to get married, he called and asked me to do the wedding. I said, "I would be honored. What did your Dad say when you told him you were getting married?" Gary said, "I am going to call him next."

When people talk about how little brotherhood means, I think of my little brother and how we see each other several times a year to this day. Our children know each other now.

Being in a fraternity saved me from loneliness and kept me from dropping out of school. It introduced me to many life-long friends and gave me values to live by. When I consider how my life would have been different had those young men not come to my room that Friday, I can not imagine it. When I talk to students today about recruitment, I tell them that somewhere out there is a potential member who needs what we have ... brotherhood and sisterhood. If they get it then their lives will be rich in the fellowship we share. If not their lives will be truly poorer in quality and enjoyment. Our heritage and ritual are our inspiration. We have an ethical imperative to share it with others. Some young man and young woman's success is depending on it. The miracle is the relationship between brother and brother and sister and sister. I thank God that a group of men reached out to me. Who are you going to approach on behalf of your brotherhood and sisterhood? If not you, then whom? If not now, when? Do it today! ★

Classmates, Friends, Sisters
by Kristen K. Brumbergs

After I accepted my invitation to attend Miami University, the next question I always got was, "So are you going to rush a sorority?" At that point in time, I had no clue. I thought sororities were for snotty girls who were stuck-up and rich. My opinion changed throughout my first semester as a freshman.

On the first day of class at this huge university, I was scared. I did not know very many people, and I desperately needed to make some good friends. So I was going to walk into my management class, look around, find the nicest person to sit by. Then I walked into the room early since I did not want to be late. Well, I saw this other girl who was sitting by herself, reading a student newspaper. She looked really kind, so I asked if anyone was sitting next to her and she said no, so I sat down. This was probably one of the best decisions I made all semester. On that first day, we talked for a few minutes before the professor got there, and I found out her name was Kelly. She was a sophomore from Cincinnati and in a sorority.

Throughout the semester, I was always excited to go to my management class because Kelly was there, and we had a good time talking before class. Both of us got to class early just so we could talk. We talked about everything, and I felt so comfortable talking to her even though she was older than me. We developed a good friendship and studied together. We even eyed the cute baseball player across the room together. She always asked me if I was going to rush, and I told her I didn't think so. Well, she made it her conquest to convince me be a part of the Greek community.

I did not know any of the Greek letters nor did I know what they looked like. Kelly would wear her letters to class, but I could never remember. She told me all the stories about Greek life and what her sorority meant to her. She told me about the sisterhood, the philanthropies, the service, and everything else she could possibly tell me. I was starting to become interested in joining one of these sororities. She told me that rush started after Christmas break, and she explained the whole process.

After talking with Kelly throughout the semester, I decided that I wanted to be a part of this wonderful Greek experience she was having. This was a decision I made on my own, since my two best friends from the dorm were not rushing.

I went home for break and tried to learn the Greek letters. There was no luck. I couldn't even remember the sorority that Kelly was in! Well, I got back to school and the rush process began. We had to go to every sorority before we could narrow down the choices. I had gone through all but two sororities and I still had not seen Kelly. I talked with girls from other sororities, but I did not get "that feeling" for any of them. I was getting worried that I would not find a sorority for me, until I walked into the Gamma Phi Beta suite. I started talking to a few members and they were just amazing. They were just like me and so down-to-earth. They were exciting, enthusiastic, and friendly. I felt better now that I found at least one I actually liked. My time at Gamma Phi Beta was even better when I spotted Kelly across the room! Her face lit up when she saw me, too, as she tried to get through the crowd to talk to me. I was so excited to finally see her.

When we talked, she said she had been waiting for me to show up there and since this was their last party, she was worried that I had withdrawn from rush. Well, I was there and I was happy!

Rush continued and I kept going back to Gamma Phi Beta. Not because Kelly was there, but because the members were the kind of people I wanted to be friends with. The time came when we had to pick which sorority we wanted, and then the sororities selected the members they wanted. Sometimes they matched up, sometimes not. So each girl picked her top three. My top one was definitely Gamma Phi Beta, without a doubt. If they did not pick me and I were to be in a different sorority, I would be crushed and not want to do it. Gamma Phi Beta was the only one I loved.

Bid day came, and I received my envelope. I was scared. I opened it very slowly, afraid of rejection. Once I saw those Gamma Phi Beta letters, my eyes filled with tears. I was the happiest girl alive! We went to the Gamma Phi Beta suite and met all of the members. Kelly was the first one I saw when I walked in, and she ran to me and gave me the biggest hug. She said she was so glad I had chosen Gamma Phi Beta, because if I hadn't she was going to be upset with me!

After a few weeks, we picked our 'Bigs', and of course I picked Kelly. From that day on we were inseparable. We did everything together. She introduced me to all of her friends and we had so much fun. She was the best friend I had needed at school. I went to her with every problem I had and she came to me. Boy, did we have problems! We took a trip to Daytona, Florida one summer and visited each other over summer break. We even ended up living two doors from each other in an apartment complex during my junior year.

We were talking one day about how we met, and she told me how she tried to convince me to be a Gamma Phi Beta. She said she purposely wore her letters all the time to class and kept telling them to me so I would want to be one, but I didn't even notice. She then told me that when she was home for break, she told her mother there was this awesome girl from her management class that she wanted to be her 'Little.' I felt so touched that she had said that and now we really were 'Big & Little' sisters.

I couldn't ask for anything more from a sorority. Gamma Phi Beta is the heart that held me together all through college. I met the nicest people who would do anything for me at the drop of a hat, and they know I would do the same for them. Through the sorority I was able to help the community grow, as well as myself. The sorority taught me many things I do not think I would have learned without it.

I owe it all to Kelly, for she is the one who really convinced me to go Greek. If it weren't for that first day of class, when I decided to sit by her, I would never have these wonderful memories, friends, or experiences. So remember, the person that you sit next to in class may end up being your best friend. You never know what you will learn from them, or what your futures will hold together. ★

The Bond of Brotherhood
by Gary D. Ballinger

When I entered college I didn't know exactly what was in store for me, but I did know that no matter what, I was not going to join a fraternity. My view of Greek life had been twisted and built upon that of the late night news stories on hazing, the pompous fraternity men from the movies, and the drunken boys from Animal House. Midway through my first semester, I realized my view might be a little skewed by the negative stereotypes, and decided to answer an ad that mentioned a new fraternity was being established on campus. Needless to say, I inquired about the group, met many of the brothers, and gratefully accepted my bid into Phi Delta Theta.

My deep commitment to my fraternity probably developed for any number of reasons, but if I could pinpoint one moment when I knew that I had made the right decision and would never regret it, then it would have to be the fall of my sophomore year.

The previous summer my father's cancer had relapsed, so I spent much of my summer worrying about his health and watching his body slowly deteriorate. By Christmas vacation I found myself driving to the hospital in a blizzard as my dad lay in his hospital bed with tubes running to his body, and a small audience of family surrounding him. I spent a lot of my vacation driving back and forth to the hospital, and even more time sleeping in the cramped lounge at the hospital so I could be a little closer to him.

The end of December brought about the end of the year and the realization that my father's health would not improve and within a few months he would succumb to his cancer. My

stepmother, being the fully devoted individual she is, decided
to take responsibility of his health care on herself with the aid
of the children. In early January, my father was transported
home where we had constructed a miniature replica of the hospital. I spent the remainder of my vacation at my father's
house, aiding my stepmother and pondering whether or not I
would return to college for the spring semester. Within a week
I knew the decision had been made for me and that I could not
return to college when my family needed so much help. It was
a hard decision to make, but I decided my family should be
first in my life and I should spend whatever time I had left
with my father. It was during this time I actually realized the
deep devotion and love my stepmother had for my father, and
my admiration of her grew as his health declined. As his health
declined, so did his memory, and slowly he would look up at
me without a spark of recognition.

If the stress of my father slowly dying wasn't enough, it
was also in January when a high school classmate, in a fit of
rage, entered into a friend's apartment and fired his shotgun at
the people inside. His wife, who was another classmate of
mine, and another individual, were fatally wounded before he
put the gun on himself and pulled the trigger. The shock of
this tragedy shook the small community where I grew up, not
to mention my fellow classmates and myself, who a year earlier
had elected the two of them as the class couple.

I traveled the hour to attend the funeral with a friend of
mine and met with a few others for dinner afterward before
heading home. On my way home I decided I needed to stop by
the fraternity house and pick up a few more things for the
week. When I entered the house I could feel a certain amount
of tension and didn't really know what was going on. One of

my brothers approached and told me my mother had called and I needed to call her immediately. Without hesitation I ran to the phone and called.She told me my father had just passed away and I needed to get home as soon as I could. My heart sank and I didn't know what to say, except that I would be there as soon as I could. My fraternity brother, who knew something wasn't right, followed me to the phone and could tell by my reaction that the news wasn't good. "Is there anything I can do?"

I choked out a tearful, "No, I just got to get to them." I quickly packed some belongings and continued on my way to my father's house. When I entered the house, my aunts, uncles, sisters, and cousins sat solemnly around the room, consoling one another.

The following day was spent mostly with my stepmother and sisters, making the funeral arrangements and contacting other family members who had not yet been notified of my father's passing. The visitation and funeral took place in the only funeral home in the very small town where my father had lived. The evening was bitterly cold and the wait to even enter the visitation was an hour long. Some people waited outside in the elements because the building was not large enough to accommodate everyone at the same time. I stood in my position with my family in the front of the room near the casket and greeted the long line of visitors. At many times the whole scene was overwhelming and I had to excuse myself from the ordeal.

About halfway through the visitation, I looked up to see all of my fraternity brothers, several chapter alumni, and even many people I had met while active in the Greek community. This in itself was overwhelming when I realized my brothers had traveled such distance in horrible weather, and then braved the elements for at least an hour as they stood outside in the bitter cold waiting to enter. I was surprised, to say the least, that all forty of my brothers had come to support me at this time, especially since the spring semester had not even started and they had to cut their Christmas vacations short.

One would think that with all this support I would be able to keep my composure, but it was their presence that overwhelmed me, and I slowly choked back the swell of tears. It was at this time I knew without any hesitation that the beliefs, rituals, and teachings of my fraternity were all true. These men that had chosen me to be their brother were standing firm for the ideals and beliefs for which my fraternity espoused by coming to my assistance at my time of need. I knew from that moment on that I would never regret my decision to join Phi Delta Theta. I would do whatever was in my power to see to it that I would use what I had learned as a member of to live my life in a way that was honorable and worthy of all it had given me.

I owe my fraternity and my brothers a great deal, because their support is what guided me through what was a very rough passage in my life. It was their encouragement that led me to re-enroll at the university later that same week. I knew they were counting on me to fulfill my duties as a brother, and I would not let them down because I, at the very least, owed them that. I owe much of my collegiate success to my brothers for the continuous encouragement and support that earned me many honors and made me a better man, citizen, and brother. ★

Finding the Words
by Marguerite Murer

Tapping my foot with wide-open eyes, I asked Cari, the executive director of Delta Delta Delta, if she was kidding. Cari laughed as she leaned back in her chair and said, "Meg, you know you can do it." I rolled my eyes and said, "Tell me again what they want the general session topic to be for convention." "The executive board would like you to do a presentation on our founder, Sarah Ida Shaw," she explained. "We want you to help our members see that Sarah Ida Shaw was a dynamic woman that shared the same emotions as each of us ... and that her sorority was a constant source of strength throughout her life." Helplessly agreeing to the charge, I asked, "Cari, where am I going to find the words?" Cari, who knew me very well, said, "Meg, you'll find them."

After several days of flipping through old fraternity Trident magazines and history books, I had come up with nothing. Frustrated, I marched around our executive office staring mindlessly into china cabinets and bookcases. My eyes roamed over ancient china, silver serving pieces, and party favors while looking for inspiration. I smiled at the yellowed rush nametags and black and white party pictures. The antique badges sparkled against black velvet. Though I found a deep sense of history and pride, I could not find the words of Sarah Ida Shaw, our founder who was larger than life in so many of our eyes. We always referred to her in that holy tone and said her full name. Her pedestal was quite high.

Still searching, I walked over to the attic door, went upstairs, and flipped on the switch. A trunk was overflowing with vibrant rush costumes and hats. I pushed aside boxes of manuals and volunteer notebooks. Shelves were sagging under the weight of initiation equipment, rush props, and convention materials. Squeezing past columns of boxes, I made my way to the archive files. Aimlessly, I opened drawers and casually flipped through files. Chapter histories, reports, and pictures flitted by, but nothing caught my attention. House corporation and financial information was quickly passed over. Switching from drawer to drawer, I could not find what I did not know I was searching for. I had just given up hope when I came across some aged files simply labeled: Sarah Ida Shaw.

Peering into the drawer, I realized that one of the files contained many of the famous Sarah Ida Shaw speeches. From Founders' Days to chapter colonizations, her familiar words were before my very eyes. Often these messages were shared at Tri Delta gatherings. I found another file of reports and comments regarding the development of Tri Delta. Though it was rather interesting, I thought it might be too technical and not quite appeal to the heart in the way that the executive board desired.

Then I came across a file that simply read: Sarah Ida Shaw/Amy Parmalee. I knew from the history books that this was one of her dear friends and sisters in Tri Delta. Opening the file, I smiled as I realized it contained a treasure trove— their letters to each other.

I sat down on the floor and began to read. In one letter, Sarah Ida Shaw was telling Amy about some Tri Delta collegians that had just visited. *"Dear Amy"*, she wrote, *"Like so many eager students, the young aspirants had looked forward to their college courses as the crowning glory of their lives, for it was to answer all their questions, to satisfy all their longings, to open the doors to all mysteries. Deep within their hearts were truths that desired expression. Deep within their souls were reservoirs of power, as yet untapped, but surging with a demand for release. Every one of these young zealots had longed to be of some special service to womanhood, as a thank you offering, perhaps, for their own good fortune in having a college education."* (1939)

I grinned, thinking of the dynamic Tri Delta collegians that I had worked with last spring during our regional leadership conferences. These women indeed were out to be of some special service. Sarah Ida Shaw knew the power and intensity of these young women.

Flipping to another letter, I cracked up. *"Dear Amy, Helen has suggested my sending Theta Psi a picture of myself. I had thought when her letter arrived that this would be quite impossible. Just yesterday, however, in doing some special work on my files, I discovered a duplicate picture. Strangely enough, the style of dressing of the period when the picture was made has come into vogue again, and the picture will not look strange, as do often a photograph made only a few years ago. It is a lovely black dress that becomes an evening gown with the doffing of the lace coat with long sleeves that come below the knuckles of the hand."* (1904)

I just could not believe that Sarah Ida Shaw would worry about how she looked to collegians. I shook my head in laughter as I thought of my own concern on what to wear during convention.

Reading on, I realized that some things do change, however. *"Dear Amy, Have called you repeatedly without success. Called you once at Public Library, to learn you would be gone for the weekend occasion of Portland Meeting. Sent you a telegram to*

*Portland—in case my airmail did not get you—but telegraph peo-
ple reported back it was not deliverable, because you weren't at
Hotel Jefferson, which was hotel given me by Bessie Brackett.
Called last night to say letter was ready, but had no one to deliver
it to a box, so decided to hold and add a written note ... El Paso
seems miles away, but my three o'clock pm airmail letter of today
will reach you tomorrow morning at 11:30 a.m."* (1938)

Today, if Sarah Ida Shaw wanted to reach Amy, she could
have emailed, faxed, paged, or called her on her cell phone.

I burst out laughing at the next letter, realizing that some
things really do not change. Dear Amy, In 1888, no woman
made the front page. We did all the work but never got any
credit for it. (1903)

Oh, how proud she would be of our collegians and alumnae out there blazing new paths.

As I carefully placed the letters around me on the floor,
and fanned my face in the hot, dusty attic, I thought how
insightful Sarah Ida Shaw was regarding our collegiate women.
She understood the timeless passion of the collegiate student.
Yet I wondered, could she understand what Tri Delta would
mean to women after college? Could she understand that some
of us would marry while others remained single? Could she
comprehend the challenges and changes in the workplace?
Would she realize our constant need for that bond of friendship?

I found another letter that made me think of our alum
group's recent discussion about our gardens. Seems Sarah Ida
Shaw and Amy had the same ideas so long ago. *"Dear Amy, It
was so good to get the fine letter that came yesterday, telling me
about your garden plans for the new trees and shrubbery. Because I
have been so blessed as to once own a garden, I can visualize the*

beauty that is going to be yours and can rejoice with you over your expanse of flowers and fruits." (1939)

Leaning back against the cool steel file cabinet, I slowly read the next letter. *"Dear Amy, As one nears middle life one realized that one's heart must stay young or wither, that one must keep the fair or grow cynical and hard. There is nothing like this interest in the fraternity in its rejuvenating power. I know it has been an inspiration to those who were strong, a tower of refuge to those who were weak, and a very comforting ally to fall back upon when hearts are sore and lives sad. I want Tri Delta to reach out and lay her loving, helpful hands on all those who have ever been a member of her family."* (1907)

I clutched the letters to my chest, wondering how Sarah Ida Shaw knew what I would be experiencing so many years later. I had celebrated the weddings of my Tri Delta sisters and shared in their sorrows. Tri Delta had indeed many times been my inspiration and my refuge. I realized I was finding the words I was searching for.

Brushing away a tear, I once again smiled at how some things change and some things remain the same. *"Dear Amy, Hortense was here yesterday for about six hours. As I was not expecting her and as I have my cleaning woman on Saturday I was neck high in housecleaning with everything from our closet strewn all over the place when the telephone rang. Hortense is no problem as far as catering is concerned. I gave her boiled eggs, bread and butter, raspberry jam and cold water. She could have had tea or coffee, but didn't want either. If I had known of her coming I would probably have planned something more elaborate, but my larder is very limited in range."* (1913)

If Cari had dropped by my house unexpectedly she would

have found the same mess as Sarah's home. We, however, probably would have run to McDonald's instead of eating boiled eggs.

As I laughed at the silly letter, it dawned on me that I was thinking of "Sarah Ida Shaw" as simply Sarah. Somewhere along the letters she had stopped being a larger than life savior of my sorority. Instead, she became a sister, someone with whom I would like to sit down and share, not cold water, but a Diet Coke. I couldn't help but smile as I realized that Sarah worried about so many of the same things that I do—will the collegians think I look hip, how can I make my garden grow, how can I help celebrate my sisters' good news.

As I sat in a sea of letters, I wondered if my friend Sarah could have understood what Tri Delta could come to mean to members as the years slip by. Could Tri Delta possibly continue to be the powerful force that was celebrated during collegiate days and embraced midlife? Such heady goals and aspirations for a sorority. *"Dear Amy, I learned that an immediate operation was imperatively necessary. I was quite alone and without relatives. There were friends aplenty, but they were scattered over the country. There was only one to whom I could turn in that hour of need, and that one was Mrs. Hortense Hudson. She came at once. Not only did she come at once, but she came prepared to stay as long as necessary. Not only did she come to stay as long as necessary, but she came prepared to do everything that a human brain could conceive or a human heart anticipate. Not only did she come prepared to do all this, but she came prepared to demand of the surgeon's permission to be present at the operation. Again and again she was refused. Again and again was she told that it was against hospital rules. At least she carried her point by the very earnest way in which she explained how deeply she felt her responsibility."* (1939)

Staring at the elegant handwriting, it was as if my friend Sarah was looking over my shoulder showing me the true power of sisterhood.

Misty eyed, I turned to the final letter in the folder. *Dear Amy, Sages have always assured us that the white light of truth can dispel the darkest night; saints have always declared that the glory of life is to serve, not to be served; and now in our day come the scientists with proof that the light from a distant star can set in motion the wheels of a dynamo and flood the world with light. Delta Delta Delta is the lining, the lever, that can bring miracles to pass through contact with the light from our stars. More and more do I want our girls to realize that there is the Kingdom and the power and the glory because of the stars above their heart, which merely await a finger-tip touch to swing them into action and fill the world with joy and good will."* (1937)

In that final letter, I realized that Sarah Ida Shaw recognized the immense potential within each member to serve. Her visions and her dreams were not something for a decade or a generation. Her visions and dreams were for all time. She knew that together, within us was the power to change the world. Gathering up my treasured letters, I knew I had found the words. ★

You Are In It For Life
by Chris Juhl

Being Greek in college was something I had always wanted to do. Regardless of stereotypical movies and bad press, I viewed joining a "frat" as a status symbol. I won't lie. I was very skeptical of the process of joining, but I kept reminding myself of the parties and women I would meet.

Needless to say, I dove in head first and joined the first chapter I had contact with; not that this was a hasty decision. Anyone who knows me would say that I am not afraid to ask questions and I did. I probably wasn't asking the right questions, but I received answers to questions I felt were important. In the end, the men of the chapter were genuine and my personality was similar to many of theirs.

After moving to college, living with my new fraternity brothers and going out to parties, I missed my first college class. I asked myself if I was doing my future any favors. Part of me thought this was great, but the other part knew I had to watch myself. I made a commitment to try harder to be successful. After a few weeks of classes, homework, and fraternity business, I still had doubts about school and doubts about when I would have to start swallowing goldfish and making panty runs to local sororities. I didn't fear all-out hazing. I trusted myself. If I felt as though I was placed in a compromising position, I would drop out. As days went by, I was learning that fraternity life had much more to offer than parties and women.

Then it was brought to the attention of our new member class that we needed to raise money for a pledge class road-trip.

There was a local alumnus who allowed younger members of our chapter to come to his house and do odd jobs, such as raking leaves or cleaning windows, for money. We arranged a time to go over to his house and do some work for him. Little did I know what was to come from this visit.

Early on a fall Saturday morning (early as far as Greek students are concerned) myself and six of my associate class brothers went over for what was setting up to be a long day. Once we reached the address, we rolled out of our cars and walked up to the front door. Many of us noticed the size of the lawn and the number of trees from which leaves had fallen. As we approached the door, an older white-haired gentleman greeted us and invited us in. Most of us entered, while a few who needed their early morning fix of nicotine stayed outside. I was upset at this because I felt it was rude to our host. I later realized this mattered very little to our host, who knew how college students were even fifty-some years after he had graduated.

As we entered the kitchen, he introduced us to his wife. She herself was an alumnus of a sorority on campus, which is how the two of them met. She was busy preparing refreshments for us. After quick introductions and a tour of his house, he explained what needed to be done, where we could find the equipment to do it, and how he suggested we tackle our duties.

After a couple of hours of laboring under his watchful eye and his entertaining company, his wife called us in for a break. It was nothing fancy, but nonetheless thoughtful and well received, even though a few members of the group were less than thrilled to be doing manual labor. She had prepared juice, hot chocolate, sandwiches, fruit, and cookies for us. I believe this made us feel a little guilty and willing to work harder on our chores. Some of our class had to leave soon after, and the rest of us stayed to complete the work.

After four hours of work we were tired and ready to go home. We enjoyed our visit and were grateful for the opportunity to raise money for our future adventures. We were worried about how much money we would get paid, since half of the guys left early and it took us an hour longer to finish the work. We were hoping for about seventy-five dollars for labor that really wasn't hard, considering the effort we had put in. After the last task was completed, he handed me a check. He thanked us for our time and let us know how much he and his wife appreciated our chapter helping them out. Not wanting to seem greedy, I didn't look at the check until we pulled away from their house.

We filed back into the car and headed for home. Dying to know how much we made, I pulled out the check and unfolded it. I opened it and said out loud, "One hundred ninety dollars?" Shock, awe, and amazement ran over my face at once. We were elated. We had hoped to raise two hundred dollars for our trip, and on our first effort we received all we needed. I remember immediately thinking this was the definition of commitment and he was a model for what an alum should be and what I, as a new member, needed to strive for.

When we returned home we were asked how the day had gone and what we thought of this particular alum. The majority of our conversation revolved around how much money he had given us, but we also talked about his interest in us, asking questions about who we were and where we came from. Older members laughed because they saw the enthusiasm and excitement in our eyes that they once had. They were not surprised by our comments or by the donation he had made. They explained this was not the first time he had made such a generous gift to the chapter. My first encounter with my new fraternal role model was not his first encounter with a member of our chapter.

After an up and down first semester of college, I had to make the decision of whether or not to return. I ended up leaving and grew further apart from my fraternity brothers than I had ever thought possible. After about nine months and some quality time defining myself as an individual, I resumed contact with my chapter before moving back to the house. I had a new perspective on life and was committed to the chapter. Along with the faded memory of an alumnus and the support of my chapter, I was determined to rise to the top and have an affect on all I came in contact with.

I began to wonder what had happened to the alumnus who made such an impression on so many people. I had a feeling of wariness. Had I let him down? Would he remember me? Would he want to see or speak with me? To say the least, I had an anxious uneasiness about it.

Once spring rolled around, we received a call from Polly McGinnis, the wife of Dallas McGinnis. They were wondering if we had a group of men who were able to come over and help with spring cleaning. This was my chance. I accompanied a group of new members who had never met the McGinnis'. The nervousness set in immediately as we approached their front door. We were greeted by Dallas, the same as he did a year-and-a-half earlier, and probably the same way he has every time chapter members come over to help out. One feeling I will never forget was when Dallas said, "Well, hello Chris, it is good to see you again." Dallas McGinnis may never have heard me tell him how much that meant to me, even though I continued to accompany future new members to the McGinnis' residence, but somehow I know he knows how I feel.

About a year-and-a-half later, Mr. McGinnis died. I was torn apart and did not know how to react. I went to the wake and the funeral. At the funeral I realized how much this man had meant to me. Although I had not cried at the funerals of two great-grandparents and three grandparents, I shed tears at Dallas' funeral. I was selfish. I wanted him to be there every semester for our new members, so they could feel the way I felt when Dallas and I first met. I realized if he meant this much to me, then think of how much he must have meant to his family. I immediately said a prayer for them. When I returned home, I knew he knew what he meant to me even though I had never told him.

Dallas McGinnis is my definition of what it means to be "in it for life". Whenever possible, I tell people of my encounters with him. Even though some of the details have faded, the feelings I have will always be there. ★

My Cousin, My Sister
by Jamie Zisow

I came to Towson University expecting a normal college career, but little did I know my experience would be far from normal. My cousin, Laura, was a member of the AOPI and told me I should rush a sorority. Soon after meeting the sisters of AOPI, I fell in love with their warmth and love for one another. My road was slowly beginning to unfold in front of me as I began pledging AOPI.

Our families had always been close, but Laura was three years older than me, so we never really bonded. She had shown me the way through my high school halls when I was a freshman and she was a senior. Once again Laura would be leading the naïve freshman throughout the halls, but this time they would be the halls of sisterhood and AOPI. Laura was my new member educator, or my pledge mom throughout this trying time in my life. Her generosity amazed me, but I couldn't understand why she was doing this for me. She opened her arms and let me into her sorority and her life. At one of the first new member sleepovers, Laura looked into my eyes as I spoke of our grandmother's death. Her eyes looked dead into mine and we both cried, but smiled at the same time. Our bond was beginning to form.

Laura looked after me throughout those eight weeks of pledging and kept telling me how much AOPI was inside of me, and how much my light shined through to the sisters. I always doubted myself and couldn't understand how these seventy-five girls could know me so well. AOPI were just letters on a girl's chest to me. How could I possibly be AOPI? But

Laura kept me strong and confident.

Initiation arrived slowly but surely, and there I stood, all of the sudden a sister of AOPI … I was amazed at what I heard and saw before me. As I sat outside staring up at the sky with tears of joy running down my face, Laura came up to me and said three of the most beautiful words I had ever heard. "Congratulations, Sister Jamie Zisow."

Sister Jaime Zisow … I had finally done it. I was a sister. And Laura was there by my side the whole time. She is not only my cousin. Laura is my sister for life. Wherever we are— family dinners, funerals, social events—Laura is always there with a smile on her face looking me dead into my eyes. She is the epitome of AOPI. She has lead me down another important road in my life and given me a friendship I will cherish forever. I know I have thanked her before, but I'd like to say to her again, Thank you sister Laura Green, I love you. ★

What "*Animal House*" Never Taught Me
by Anthony J. D'Angelo

It is true the movie "*Animal House*" has shaped many a
young mind,
Yet for most men considering fraternity life the impression
is quite unkind.
You see what the video screen shows us is a big farce,
For within it, the true meaning about Greek Life is
very, very sparse.
Some might think it cool to drive a motorcycle up the stairs
Yet in the long run people who do that spend life working
state fairs.
Go ahead Bluto and stuff your face in the cafeteria line,
But don't come groveling to me when your health is not
doing so fine.
You too can wear this shoe if you think it is a fit.
Yet most of the world would not be impressed if you said
"Look I'm a Zit!"
For what Animal House forgets to tell us goes oh so
much deeper,
But to show real Greek Life in a movie would turn out to be
quite a sleeper.
You see the true meaning of being a Fraternity man cannot be
crammed in a two-hour slot,
For being Greek is a microcosm of life, in that, in order to get
through it you must learn a lot.
The lessons learned are so much different than those learned
in class,

For you will only truly come to understand this when you look
beyond the glass

No one ever told me one of my brothers would become a slave
to a bottle of beer

He would tell me "I'm okay!", but I could see through him as
he tried to drown his fear.

Or how my fraternity would rally around this one and bring
his fears to ease

As we all joined to help him overcome his dreaded alcoholic
disease.

To be involved in my chapter gave me such a sense of pride

For I was surrounded with close knit friends within whom I
could confide.

I never knew way back then, that these guys would be friends
for all my life.

Or that my brothers would be there for me the day I married
my wife.

I went in just a boy, only dreaming about girls and thirsting for
a cold black and tan

But as I left that old house on graduation day I realized that I,
I had become a man.

Going Greek is like anything in life, you can take the word of
others or find out for yourself

No silly movie will do it for you, not even Santa Clause and
his elf.

If you do have the courage to find out on your own, you will
see what is false and what is really true.

But through your own experience you will come to find the
greatest lessons are those that lie inside of you. ★

Pass It On
Author Unknown

I almost dropped out of rush.

From the time I first visited Allegheny College in the spring of my senior year of high school, I was interested in Greek life. As my host walked me through the halls of Brooks Hall, I stopped to read the poems hung neatly on the walls outside the doors of the freshman women pledging sororities. Their promises of eternal friendship and sisterhood, affectionately signed "(Greek Letter) and all of mine," intrigued me. I wanted to know how that felt.

But I nearly talked myself out of it.

I'd made friends with the girls who lived on my hall. They weren't interested in sorority life. I don't need to buy my friends, they said. I didn't really believe that, but I almost let them convince me. Then I met the sisters of Alpha Delta Pi.

They were different. I could tell from the moment I set foot in their suite. Each woman, I could see, was an individual. They were softball players, theater majors, and pre-med students. They were dancers, singers, and members of the activities board. I felt at home. I didn't feel like I had to be someone else to make them like me. I saw friendly faces from some of my classes, and my shyness melted away.

But still, I almost dropped out.

"What about the money?" I asked myself. Concerned about costs, I tried to convince myself I didn't need a sorority. I had friends. I was happy.

Then I was convinced to attend the third night of formal rush. The ADPi's had a theme party: Pi Rock Café. They wore matching "Pi Rock" shirts and served soda in old-style Coke bottles. "Records" hung on the walls and rock music played in the background.

I was greeted by Amy Jo, a girl I recognized from my dance class. We had never really talked, but I soon found that it didn't matter to AJ. She swept me around the room, making sure everyone met me. She introduced me as "the girl who taught the Electric Slide" to Jan, our dance teacher.

We sat through the slide show the chapter had prepared. Amy Jo enthusiastically described each slide, each event the chapter took part in. There were shots of philanthropy events, of social functions, and shots of sisters just "hanging out" together. I envied them.

When it was time to leave, Amy Jo hugged me. "I'm so glad you came," she said. I knew she meant it.

I was hooked. I wanted to be an ADPi.

And still, I almost talked myself out of going back. Ashley, a girl who lived down the hall who I wasn't even close with, convinced me to go. When I said I didn't have anything to wear, she loaned me a dress. "You can always decide not to pledge," she told me.

So I returned for the fourth night Preference Party. I was again greeted by an only slightly familiar face. Jennifer (JJ to her friends) had apparently picked me out of the crowd of freshmen. "That girl is cool," she'd told her friends. "She's going to be my little."

During the fourth night ceremony, each sister read something to the rushee she'd been paired with—a poem or a personal message. It seemed that all the other pairs knew each other well. I was worried. But when it was JJ's turn, she set my mind at ease. She told me how special I was, made be feel like I belonged. Then she hugged me, and led me to the diamond-shaped puzzle in the middle of the room. She pulled out one of the pieces, and handed it to me. "A piece of A D Pi" it said, with my name underneath it.

The puzzle, we were told, represented each individual in the chapter; how each individual helped make up the whole.

We stood in a circle then. The president of the chapter started a candle pass, passing it once around the room as a symbol of friendship. As the candle made its way around the room, the sisters sang their own words to the hymn "Pass It On." "What a happy house is this, when we are all together. As sisters we exist, we live for one another," the chapter sang.

My eyes welled with tears. ADPi's open motto, "We Live for Each Other," was to me the ideal of friendship.

I held my preference card in my hands. I had attended two preference parties, but I knew what I wanted to do. Although the rush counselors advised against it, I wrote "ADPi" on the card, leaving the other spaces blank. It was a practice they commonly referred to as "intentional single preferencing." If ADPi didn't offer me a bid, I wouldn't be in a sorority at all. I didn't care, because I didn't just want to be in a sorority. I wanted to be an ADPi.

Saturday morning I waited. I had chosen. I had to wait to see if they chose me. If I were going to get a bid, the sisters would bring it to my door at one o'clock.

The enthusiastic banging on the door came at moments after one. I was hardly breathing. I opened the door, and Amy Jo pulled a letter sweatshirt over my head. I think she read the bid card. I don't remember.

I wore the letters so proudly. I was an ADPi. I had found the place where I belonged. I silently thanked Ashley for not letting me drop out.

Amy Jo and the others hugged me, then we were off. They ran with me to Brooks Circle, where the rest of the chapter was waiting. JJ was the first to hug me when we got there. "I was so worried about you," she said. Worried that I would decide not to pledge or to pledge somewhere else. There was no place else for me.

I still wear the letters proudly, even four years after I have graduated from Allegheny. My closest friends are still the ones I made as a collegiate member of Eta Beta chapter—friends that were not "bought", but made and cultivated through common experiences, deepened by the bond of sisterhood.

And the words to that song, the words I now know by heart, still bring a tear to my eye. "I'll shout it from the mountain top, I've come to ADPi. It has given me the love you see, and now I'll pass it on." ★

Recruitment vs. Rush
by Robert J. Kerr

I was a first generation college student with no thoughts of joining a fraternity. After all, fraternities were for rich kids with family connections. What could the son of a tool and die maker possibly have, besides the dues check, to interest a fraternity? Besides, I needed to figure out how to pay for the second semester of college and the thought of adding more expenses to my monthly overhead seemed foolish. So when I drove onto the University of Kansas campus to work as a counselor for the Kansas Boys State program, I was looking forward to a great week and to hopefully returning to the KU campus in the fall.

Through the Boys State week I was busy running my city and enjoying talking with the other first-year counselors. We were all comparing notes about college and about college co-eds. Then, one guy asked me which house I was going to join. I could barely stand from laughing so hard. Which house? Which fraternity house was I going to join—who was he kidding? I told him that I had no interest, no money, and besides, no fraternity had even talked to me.

The next day while eating lunch, a guy by the name of Roger came over and said hello. He introduced himself and indicated he was a student a Washburn University. He told me he understood I was considering attending Washburn and I had been offered a football scholarship. I told him yes, but hadn't made up my mind about attending. He chuckled and we chatted briefly. He then excused himself and we both went about our business. The week sped by and then the Governor's Ball was held on Friday night. All the counselors were busy keeping the Staters and their dates out of the bushes. Roger made a point to find me and introduce himself and his date, a sorority lady from KU. I was stunned he would take the time to find me and amazed he remembered my name.

After the Governor's Ball, the next day Boys State ended for another year. It had been a great week, lots of activities, new friends, and now the excitement of new adventures awaiting. As I was checking out, Roger said hello and encouraged me to stop by the fraternity house sometime or attend one of their lake parties. I thanked him and indicated I would be pretty busy working all summer. Roger shook my hand and said he would be in touch. I smiled and headed back to Wichita, thinking nothing of his statement. Then, about three weeks later, there was a call from Roger. He was in town and wanted to stop by my home and talk. I agreed.

Roger arrived at my family's home in a neat pair of white trousers, and a white golf shirt with the fraternity crest on the breast pocket. As I let Roger in, he smiled and shook my hand and then introduced himself to my mother and father. I had him now. No way was he going to convince my folks to let me join a fraternity. Then I would not have to excuse my way out of party invitations.

As I sat down I was prepared to answer all of his questions. But they never came. Roger asked my parents what they wanted me to get out of my college experience. What were their concerns, their fears, and their hopes. For over an hour Roger explained how the fraternity could support my academic program, introduce me to key people, and keep me in school. My parents listened intently. They asked questions. Roger answered. They looked at the cost and Roger explained how many members worked and they could help me find a job on campus. I was stunned at how my parents were approaching this conversation. They seemed to be genuinely interested in my belonging to this fraternity.

After an hour-and-a-half, Roger politely looked at his watch and asked to be excused. He rose and shook my mother's hand and then my father's hand. As he and I shook hands, Roger told me he hoped I would attend Washburn and would seriously consider joining his fraternity. I smiled and promised to seriously consider both situations. With that he smiled, walked to his car, and drove off. As I walked back to the house I thought, no more fraternity crap for me.

When I walked into the house my folks asked me to sit down. They wanted to know what I thought. I told them I thought he was okay but wasn't sure I wanted to go to Washburn. I had my heart set on Kansas or Missouri. They wanted to know what I thought about the fraternity. I told them I could care less. "We think you should reconsider," they said.

I couldn't believe my ears. My parents, suggesting I join a fraternity, oh my God! Before I could respond, they clarified their statement. "That is the only fraternity we will support you joining."

They had heard all the phone calls from fraternities and seen all the mail. The fact Roger was willing to drive 140 miles, sit in our house and talk to them, was something they both appreciated and respected. It was something no one else was willing to do, including those fraternities who were housed in Wichita. As a first generation student, the degree of respect and interest Roger showed was reassuring and helped me make some key decisions.

I ultimately attended Wichita State, and called Roger to tell him my decision. He understood and referred me to the chapter on the WSU campus. I made contact with them and pledged the next week. Now, thirty years later, Roger serves on the national board of directors of the fraternity and I have remained active as a volunteer for the past twenty-five years. All because one undergraduate member walked up a sidewalk, knocked on a door, and then talked from the heart with my parents. I never attended a rush event, never went to a house party, and never regretted the decision I made. Oh, Roger, Mom says Hi! ★

Inspiration for Greeks

Look Within
by Marguerite Murer

As a field consultant, I had been taught the proper rhetoric regarding rush. The Greek system creates a sct of guidelines and rules, which will allow each chapter to showcase their strengths and opportunities. The system is hypothetically designed so that in a brief time, a rushee can share some insight to their personality, potential, and dreams. Within this system, somehow young men and women are supposed to find a place to call home. Among all the balloons, songs, skits, and lemonade, I mentally understand that the Greek community does the best it can. But what happens when you are not on top? How do you show people the potential within? And how do you let people know that this can be home?

The air conditioner whirled, yet had little impact on the overcrowded basement. Metal chairs were smashed together in jagged rows, while our members sat on pillows for the lengthy night meeting. The spirit committee was busy passing around bowls of suckers and Tootsie Rolls while attempting to get the chapter to join in a song with little success. I huddled with the rush committee at the table in the front room trying to figure out how to begin our discussion. I was so proud of this tiny chapter. They were fighting valiantly for their survival in the Greek community.

On a small campus, once a chapter is pegged with a stereotype, it is difficult to change to the status quo. Tri Delta was the brainy chapter. These young women would someday find cures for rare diseases, be brilliant political leaders, and passionate humanitarians. Unfortunately, in the fraternity social pecking order, that didn't seem to matter much. Though these young women were diverse leaders in campus organizations, they lacked some of the social skills that endeared other sororities to the fraternities. At times these women were confident their day in the sun would come.

Rush seemed to take all the sunshine out of these gifted women. They understood my very presence as a field consultant signified the executive board was concerned for their future. Low numbers of women, pledged over the past several years, had this chapter shrinking at an alarming rate. I was there to offer support with firm guidance. The rush committee agreed with my opening and settled back in their chairs.

I walked around the front of the table and casually sat on top. Slowly looking at the group of fifty-plus members, I gave my most confident smile. Carefully, I began, "I am very proud and impressed with your performance today. You all radiated joy and happiness as you talked with the rushees. I could clearly see how much you all loved Tri Delta as I walked around the rooms. Listening to you describe your sisterhood activities, philanthropy events, and intramurals made me want to stay here forever."

This brought smiles to many faces. I continued on, "It was obvious that you all care deeply about each other. I could also see your pride in your chapter house. Believe me, many of your sisters across the nation would love to live in this beautiful home. I want you to know that no matter what happens tomorrow, it is clear you gave your very best today and you all should have great pride in that. I am proud to be your sister."

More grins greeted me. Taking a deep breath, I slowly said, "Tonight we need to decide who we are going to invite back for second round parties. I need you all to think very carefully and look deep within yourselves as we discuss the rushees. I want you to visualize yourselves before you joined Tri Delta and think about how it has impacted your life. For your chapter to decide not to invite someone back, there has got to be a very strong reason. For example, her grades fall below our established standards, or her behavior is completely out of sync with the beliefs and goals of our fraternity. This is no place for my boyfriend's roommate's cousin knows someone who said. We are only going to deal with firsthand knowledge."

A bold senior from the back row called out, "Are you saying that we have to invite every single person back for second round parties?" I knew this was coming. Calmly, I said, "No, I'm saying we need to carefully consider every single person. If you all decide to not invite someone back, there needs to be a really strong reason." "So we still have a choice? You are not going to force us into automatically inviting everyone back?" "You still have a choice," I said.

This seemed to calm down the steaming members. As I looked at their hurt eyes I wanted to wave a magic wand and make it all better. I knew their frustration came not from me, but from fighting the stereotypes and campus images. They were hurt that others did not want them. This was the part of the Greek community that was so painful.

A timid sophomore raised her hand, looked me square in the eye and asked, "Why don't they like us?" I felt my heart break and said, "You cannot listen to what other people say or worry about what the rushees are going to do. Those that know you like you so much, just like me. Sometimes it is hard for people to move past a stereotype. Your challenge during rush is to move people past the images so they get to know the real you. When they get to know you, they like you. Also, you can't worry about who likes you. I know that might not help the hurt, but instead focus on the people that do care about you. Every single person in this room cares about each other. The people on campus that you lead and interact with in your organizations all care about each of you. And someday you all are going to change the world."

Wanting to believe me, everyone settled into their chairs, ready to begin our discussion.

Time passed slowly as we discussed the endless list of rushees. Occasionally, a member would speak passionately about how impressed they were with a particular rushee. Listing off the young women's many activities and good grades, I could tell the chapter was impressed. Just as quickly, though, the member would sit down as if realizing that the rushee would probably pledge a "top" chapter. How I wanted to give them hope. We were already in the middle of the alphabet before a severe grade risk appeared. Though Julie was a dynamic freshman, it was clear she did not take school too seriously. The chapter recognized that a cornerstone of their chapter was their commitment to academic excellence. After a brief discussion, they decided to not invite Julie back. It seemed to relax them that they still had a choice in who was attending their rush parties.

Members began squirming in their chairs, while others fanned themselves with the long lists of rushees. The heat was dampening our spirits and the chapter was slipping into a pit of frustration. Peggy, the rush chairman, brought up the next rushee, Erica, for discussion. At first there was not much conversation. From what we knew, Erica was involved in her high school, had good grades, and seemed rather shy. Suddenly a voice broke out from the back row blasting, "I didn't get a good feeling from her. I think we should not invite her back." I heard the challenge in Amy's voice and stood up to see her face. There was a defensive look in her eye, and I was worried that this really had nothing to do with Erica. Diane, a tender-hearted sophomore, whirled around in her chair and said to Amy, "I liked her a lot. She was involved in a lot of things and I think she would be an asset to this chapter. She seemed sincere when she told me she was looking for a place to belong." Amy snarled back, "Well, I didn't feel that way. Besides, I am a senior and I have more experiences with rush than you do."

With that the chapter broke in two, and comments were hurled fast and furious. Trying to gain control, I yelled for order. It took several attempts before the upset women finally calmed down. I explained that we would have to vote on this invitation since the chapter was so upset. I gave my best speech about looking at the potential of every person. It wasn't good enough. With a close vote, the chapter decided not to invite sweet Erica back for the next round of parties. I closed my eyes in defeat. This wasn't about Erica. This was about some members feeling the need to reject someone because so many other people had rejected them. A dull quietness fell over the chapter, and the rest of the meeting passed with little discussion. Exhausted, they went off to sleep.

I was impressed with their ability to rebound over the next several days. With chins lifted in determination, they bravely faced the list of low returns each day. Instead, they focused on the small number of women who returned to their chapter. They sang their hearts out and shared their sisterhood. With timid smiles they explained time and again what made their chapter special, hoping to reach past the campus images. While lighting their candles during preference parties, my heart once again went out to them. Oh, how they wanted people to join them. If only people would look within and see what they were offering. After the parties, they warmly accepted my compliments and praise for their dedication and persistence. They knew they had something special in their chapter.

As the field consultant, I participated in the bid matching process. Electricity filled the air as the perky Kappa Kappa Gamma advisor passed around bagels. The confident Delta Gamma advisor offered me orange juice while patting my arm soothingly. It was easy for them to be so happy-go-lucky. They knew they would take quota right away with all of the top rushees. I was just praying to pledge at least half of quota. As we all settled in around the long wood table, advisors exchanged cute little stories from the past few days.

Papers were shuffled into neat piles as sharp pencils were passed around. The procedure was quickly reviewed and the list of those dropping out of rush was read. Suddenly rushee names were being called out. Molly — Delta Gamma. Match. Jessica — Kappa Kappa Gamma. Match. Michelle — Pi Beta Phi. Pass. She will remain in the stack.

The names rolled on while I waited and waited to hear Delta Delta Delta. My heart still hurt. Yet it is an interesting process to be a part of. As certain rushee names were called, advisors gave little yelps of joy, knowing their members would be excited, while other advisors let out little sighs of disappointment when a favorite rushee pledged another house. Then the advisors get excited for each other and cheer each other on.

When the Greek advisor called out Dawn— Delta Delta Delta,
and I said 'match', everyone cheered for me. They understood
how important each rushee was to our chapter.

We marched through the names to the beat of match,
match, pass, match, pass, and so on. After Missy was matched
to Kappa Kappa Gamma, the advisor cheered quota. We all
clapped for her. Several other groups quickly followed her lead.
The Greek advisor turned over the final stack of cards and
explained that we would go through the stack one more time.
Some of the cards were single preference. A few of the foolish
women were matched to only the sorority they had listed.
Several more were not, thus they would not be pledged by any
chapter. The Greek advisor reminded us again that we must
continue to stress and educate that single preference bidding
for rush often ends in heartache.

With that speech over, she picked up the one remaining
card and said, "I have one young woman left who would like to
belong somewhere. From what I understand, she is a sweet person who has good grades and was involved in high school. In a
sense she has fallen through the cracks. She was not high
enough on the various chapters' bid list to be pledged. Those of
you that have not reached quota, would you be interested in
pledging her?" The room filled with an uncomfortable silence.
Two other chapters declined. The Greek advisor turned to me.
I asked if I could have ten minutes. After she nodded yes, I
sprinted across campus back to the chapter house.

Flying into the house, I rang the dinner bell, indicating an
emergency meeting in the formal living room. Still panting, I
motioned for everyone to be seated. They warily looked at me
as I tried to regain my breath. Anxious eyes wanted to know

what had happened. Carefully I explained that it was still in progress and that it was going fairly well. They relaxed at that, since fairly well is better than fairly bad.

Taking a deep breath I began, "We have a situation with a rushee. She has been cut out of rush since some of the other groups have already filled to quota. This young woman truly wants to be Greek. She wants to find a place to call home. A place to find sisters. A place where she can grow as an individual as well as helping the chapter."

They were staring at me intently. I continued, "I want you all to think about what your life was like before you joined this sorority. Then I want you to think about how you have changed. I can tell you that I am a far better person because of Tri Delta. I have learned so much about being a team player, about believing in common goals, about being a leader, about making sacrifices, about being a friend. I can't imagine how different my life would be without Tri Delta. Luckily someone saw the potential in me. Just like someone saw the potential within each of you."

Standing a little taller, I said, "Erica needs a place to call home." Eyes popped open and mouths dropped. Immediately Amy said, "But we didn't invite her back. How in the world could we pledge her?" "The Greek advisor said we could give her our open rush process," I said. "She would join our pledge class today and be a part of everything right from the start. What do you all think?" They were quiet for several moments, each lost in thought. Finally Amy said, "I'm lucky someone believed in me. I would be honored to have her as a sister." Everyone else chimed in their agreement and I found myself sprinting back across campus.

Inspiration for Greeks

Knocking on Erica's door, I hoped I would find the right words. The Greek advisor and I had had a long chat about how best to approach the situation. A warm smile greeted me as I introduced myself. Erica invited me in and asked me to sit down. I carefully explained that Tri Delta would like to invite her to become a member. Confused, she asked how, since she had not been invited back after the first round of parties. I said that sometimes things happen that we cannot fully explain or even understand. I quietly told her how Tri Delta had positively impacted my life over the years and how I was a better person because of my involvement. I continued that the chapter did want her to become a member because they believed in her and wanted her to be a part of their chapter. I asked her to look within herself and think about if she really wanted to be a part of a sorority. If so, I asked her to give Tri Delta a chance and to come to the house this afternoon for the Bid Day celebration.

As I sat on the front porch watching eager new members receive blue Tri Delta tee-shirts, my eyes kept drifting toward the sidewalk. Silver, gold, and blue balloons swayed in the wind, while Tri Delta chants filled the air. Then I saw her slowly walking toward the house. Amy spotted her, too, and rushed forward with a tee-shirt. "Erica, we are so glad you are home."

My heart was light as I watched them hug. At the time I did not know Erica would become a brilliant leader. She would inspire her pledge class to be bold and inviting to everyone on campus. That she would become the chapter's dynamic social chairman as a sophomore. She would make an immense difference because she was willing to look within. I only knew she had finally found her home. ★

It Pays To Be Greek
by Theresa D. Chandler

My story is not a touching memory that will bring a tear to the eye. It is a story about how being Greek has affected my professional life. It is one of those benefits that never entered my mind as being an advantage when I was a collegian. Of course, most of us really did not bother to look beyond our college days to what it would mean to be a Greek alumna. Here's my story.

In the spring of 1999, I decided to look for another job, as my current employment situation had become undesirable. Therefore, I began exploring my options. I applied for an interesting position that not only combined my two college degrees as well as my minor course of study, but also my work experience. I felt I had the perfect background for this new position. I was granted an interview and was told that second round interviews would be conducted the following week by the CEO, who was coming to town just for that purpose. My vacation was scheduled for the following week, and I explained this to the interviewer. I offered to make myself available via telephone for the CEO, but was told that was not necessary.

When I returned from my vacation, I promptly phoned the person with whom I interviewed and was told the position was already filled and all that remained was for her references to be checked. I expressed my disappointment and mentioned I was still very interested in the job. She told me she had resigned with the company but would pass that information on to the upper management.

Two days later, I had a message on my answering machine

from the out-of-state company director to which this position would report. I returned the call and expressed my surprise, because I had been told the position was filled. This director stated that the other person had not been acceptable to her and she would like to talk with me over the telephone. I believe my education and experience got me this telephone interview.

However, the primary conversation centered around my volunteer experience from my Greek organization that I had joined while in college. In the twenty-plus years since college, I have been a volunteer in various capacities for Alpha Omicron Pi. My most recent involvement has been as a recruitment (rush) network specialist for several collegiate chapters. My duties have included providing training, seminars, and programs in the areas of recruitment, public relations, and Panhellenic development.

After several minutes of conversation about this volunteer job and others that I have held over the years for Alpha Omicron Pi, I was told I would be hearing from them soon.

The next day I received the job offer. It seems that the company director with whom I had the telephone interview was a member of Alpha Gamma Delta and identified with my commitment to AOII in addition to having a career and a family. She knew and appreciated what it took to give of myself for twenty years to something I had pledged myself to as a collegian.

I will have to say that my being Greek helped me attain my current employment position. However, it has meant much more than that to me over the years. I am truly grateful for my collegiate experience, but it has been my experience as an alumna that has meant the most.

A number of my closest friends are also Greek. They are not usually members of Alpha Omicron Pi, but of other NPC groups. In the office where I work, two of the other three women are also members of NPC groups (Alpha Delta Pi and Zeta Tau Alpha). Two of my closest friends in my community are affiliated with still other NPC groups (Alpha Gamma Delta and Phi Mu). Two of my closest male friends are also Greek (Sigma Chi and Kappa Alpha Order). Of course, I still retain a close relationship with several of my sisters with whom I shared the collegiate experience even though we do not live in the same state.

I think being a member of Alpha Omicron Pi has helped shape me into the woman that I am. Some of the attributes I gained as a collegian and have built upon as an alumna member of Alpha Omicron Pi include leadership and delegation aptitude, goal-setting abilities, interpersonal communication skills, and problem-solving skills. I am truly grateful to have had the occasion to join Alpha Omicron Pi while in college and for the opportunity it afforded me to be a part of the greater Greek community. My years of commitment as an alumna volunteer would not have been possible without the support of my husband of the last twenty-one years, who is also a member of a Greek organization (Pi Kappa Alpha). Without his understanding and assistance and that of our daughter's, I could not have given freely of my time. Being Greek has certainly opened doors for me professionally and helped me to grow professionally—but perhaps the greatest gift is the cherished friendships with members of other Greek organizations.

★

The Pebble In My Pond
by Anthony J. D'Angelo

I don't think he really knew,
Now three years later how much I really grew.

You see way back then,
All I could ask is when, when, when?

When will I get a bid?
He was there when I did.

When will I get in?
He was there to help me win.

When will I get a little of my own?
He shared the news with me over the phone.

It was my big brother who was the pebble in my pond,
For what he saw in me was all good and no wrong.

I hope and pray when the torch is passed to me,
That I too can serve my little brother, as I was by he. ★

Rose Petals
by Erin Benda Evers

"I don't like that girl. She has funny, frizzy, yellow, permy hair, and she looks like she's five. She'll be the shortest person in our class! Plus, she thinks she's so important because she's the pastor's daughter." It was the summer before fourth grade, and my mother had been encouraging me all week to introduce myself to the new pastor's daughter.

"Erin, she doesn't know anyone in Iowa City yet. How would you feel if you had to leave all of your friends and move to a new area where you didn't know anyone? Besides, you might find that you like her. Just invite her to walk home from church with you on Sunday and I'll make your favorite, grilled peanut butter sandwiches."

So, that's how it began. A forced act of kindness on my part and a couple of peanut butter sandwiches led to the most important and true friendship of my life. Though the two of us were a bit standoffish for the first five minutes, we found we had a lot in common. We both liked boys, summer camp, boys, swimming at the local pool, boys, and shopping. At the ripe old age of ten, I had never had a friend with whom I had so much in common. I quickly found myself spending all of my time with Kristen.

Within a week, Kristen presented me with a note marked "TOP SEEKRIT". Inside she'd written, "I think it's time that we be best-friends. Check a box." Below she'd drawn two boxes, one marked "yes" and one marked "no". I checked "yes".

Kristen's father was the minister of our small Lutheran church for the next four years. During this time, Kristen's family and mine seemed to become meshed into one large family. Kristen and I came to feel more like sisters than close friends. We liked to pretend we were twins and often convinced our moms to buy us identical outfits, but in different colors, so we could attempt to pull off the twin sister act in front of our other friends. Our parents allowed us to be involved in all the same activities such as softball, piano lessons, swim team, summer camp, and Sunday School.

We no longer spoke of our parents as separate sets of people. Instead we spoke of "the moms" who were in the kitchen talking and "the dads" who were outside barbecuing. We spent more time together than apart. For instance, a week did not go by that our families didn't go out to dinner together. A day did not go by that our moms didn't talk on the phone about "the girls". We even liked to fantasize about my sister and her brother, who were the same age, becoming married someday so that we could become "real by-law sisters". Somehow, even at our young age, we knew that we were meant to be sisters.

One day, toward the end of seventh grade, I returned home from school to find my mother sitting at the kitchen table crying while my father was trying to console her. They broke what seemed to be the worst of all possible news. Kristen's father had accepted a call to another church that would take their family nearly three hours from our town. We felt as though our worlds had been shattered. But we vowed that no matter what happened, no matter where we were in the world, no matter what other friends came into our lives, we would always be the closest of friends. We kept this vow to the end.

Through the next five years, our families kept in close contact. Kristen and I were allowed to visit each other for extended visits over school breaks. So, during our senior year of high school, it came as little surprise to our parents when we broke our news to them that we would be attending Coe College together in the fall of 1995.

Orientation week at Coe College was meant to help students adjust to major lifestyle changes before adding the challenge of classes. As Kristen and I unpacked and looked out the window across the quadrangle at other dorms, we saw students happily greeting each other. One thing became very clear to us: the real orientation to college life was about meeting friends. This was achieved mainly by partying. But as a shy freshman, I wondered how I was ever going to muster up the courage to leave our newly familiar dorm room and walk into a party of strangers.

As Kristen was encouraging me to "hurry up" there was a knock at the door. There stood several upperclassmen, wearing tee-shirts with huge letters reading "A – O - TT". They asked us if we'd like to walk over to a party with them. As we made the party rounds that night, we got to know these girls better.

Kristen and I were struck by their close friendships and camaraderie. They talked about their sorority and the fun times they shared at special celebrations when someone became engaged. But they also talked about the many opportunities to contribute to the lives of each other and the community. Jenn told us about reading to kids in the pediatric unit of a nearby hospital. Raquel talked about the annual teeter-totter-athon fundraiser for arthritis research. Then even talked about days spent cleaning up the highway as if it wasn't work, but merely doing something for society while hanging out with their very best friends.

I was especially impressed by the way these women helped Megan through her last semester with a broken arm. By rotating turns to help Megan with the smallest of tasks, such as taking notes in classes and typing her term papers, they had allowed Megan to graduate on time. Kristen and I quickly realized that the sorority friendships were much like a family. Though we hadn't given much thought to joining a sorority, one week later we found ourselves eagerly signing our bid cards in hopes of becoming members of Alpha Omicron Pi. We knew for sure that we were finally headed toward a true form of sisterhood. Little did we know how truly important the sorority sisterhood was to become in our remaining time together.

Within a few weeks, Kristen and I were beginning to settle into our new lives as college students. We were both keeping up in our classes, enjoyed studying together and attending Greek functions with our new friends.

One evening, this all changed forever. Kristen returned home from a particularly difficult swim team practice with agonizing abdominal pains. Several hours later, when the pain had not subsided, I took Kristen to the nearest emergency room, where she was examined and given an ultrasound. I was invited into the room to watch the procedure because of my interest in medicine. I distinctly remember the nervous expression on the young resident's face when a dark mass appeared on the screen where there should only have been abdominal space. At this point, the young resident sharply asked me to wait outside.

Kristen wasn't to return home to our dorm room that night. Kristen wasn't to return to our dorm room ever. Kristen was diagnosed with a rare form of cancer. Her treatment required that she return to her hometown for the remainder of her life, two years.

I felt so helpless to do anything for her during the worst moments of her illness. I could not help her the day I found her ripping clumps of her long blonde hair from her head because it had begun to fall out and was making her scalp itch. I could not help her during physical therapy when she struggled with her loss of coordination making it difficult for her to place her heal down before her toe as she tried to walk. I could not help her to resent her death any less when she received the news that her physicians had ran out of options to treat her.

However, there were many times when our sisterhood did help, and for this I'm thankful. My sisters continually renewed Kristen's and my strength to fight for her life because we knew that fifty girls cared about us and wanted to see her live. Every weekend some of my sisters made the three-hour trip to visit Kristen in the hospital, even if it meant staying the night on the lobby couches. Every week they sent her some sort of fun package such as the ugliest hats we could all come up with to keep her bald head warm. These included paper sailor hats, tie-dyed hats, clown wigs, or colorful handkerchiefs.

There is one memory I have surrounding Kristen's illness that always brings tears to my eyes. One of my sisters came to Kristen's funeral carrying a red Jaqueminot rose, the flower of our sorority, for each of us to remind us that AOTT is for a lifetime, as is our sisterhood and support of one another. Another sister came carrying a white rose for each of us, Kristen's favorite flower. When I close my eyes, I can still hear the church bells echo in the afternoon silence while my sisters and I lined the sidewalk outside the church as Kristen passed us in her casket for the last time. I remember shivering, though the summer sun was warm on my shoulders, as we each dropped a red and white rose pedal behind her. That's how I will remember saying goodbye to my best friend ... red and white rose petals in the summer sun completely surrounded by my sisters. ★

Why Not?

by Leslie Ervin Trahant

People often ask me why I stay involved in my sorority. I have a simple answer—why not? Why not continue the bonds of sisterhood that I enjoyed during college? Why not challenge myself to take on projects and to learn new skills? Why not meet incredibly strong and bright women from across the country? Why not share experiences with women who are twice my age or half my age? Why not revel in the joy of watching a collegiate sister finally grasp a concept? Why not meet new friends who will take you to places of which you would have never imagined? Why not have friendships that see one another through successes, failures, laughter, tears, joys, sorrows, births, deaths, marriages, divorces, promotions, firings, sickness, and health? Why not take a day of vacation from work to attend a university disciplinary hearing for your chapter? Why not support a sister who is in an abusive relationship or has an eating disorder or a drinking problem? Why not enjoy the love and joy of shared goals and a common vision? Why not have your own personal board of directors to which you can turn in any situation and at any moment? Why not hold the hand of a sister as she buries a parent, her husband, or a child? Why not sing to a sister as she dances with her new husband at their wedding? Why not serve as a mentor for younger members? Why not get back more than you can ever imagine possible?

Why not, indeed. ★

My Perspective
by John Ashworth

I'm not sure which decision I came to first: I want to be a brother of Sigma Nu, or I want to be with Tom, a brother in Sigma Nu, for the rest of my life. Luckily for me, the decisions were not mutually exclusive. Sigma Nu is not your stereotypical fraternity on the Dartmouth College Campus, and Dartmouth is not exactly the real world. But I believe my experience proves that fraternities and sororities can provide an unparalleled environment of love and acceptance.

I wasn't open about my sexuality in my hometown in West Virginia. Before I entered Dartmouth two years ago, I had come out only to my best friend, Alyssa. She and I had done everything together in high school—even playing together on the boy's soccer team—except date. Our friends always expected us to, and her dad always said that we'd find each other after our first divorces. Since I came out to Alyssa on my 18th birthday, he doesn't believe that anymore.

Before I arrived at Dartmouth, I visualized fraternity culture as a combination of Animal House antics and country club personalities—a place where members bought their friends and networked with other rich, white boys. My flawed ideas were put to rest during orientation week when a dorm-mate, Brian, a junior, and a brother in Sigma Nu invited me over to hang out at the house. I felt completely comfortable and began to spend copious amounts of time there.

That increased after I met Tom. He is a striking man, physically and mentally. He still teases me that right after we were introduced, my eyes followed him around the room and then up the stairs. After a few weeks of thinly-veiled mutual attraction, we found ourselves in a situation where it was just the two of us and, well, it was time to admit that we were attracted to one another.

Tom was openly gay in the fraternity, and I knew the brothers would be as accepting of me. But I didn't want more on my plate that first term, so for the first month-and-a-half we dated secretly. Sometime in January I was hanging out in Tom's room at the house and it got to be late. I heard people in the corridor and knew I'd get some questioning looks if I exited then.

But it was time to put an end to the charade, so I strolled confidently from Tom's room to the stairwell, where five guys were sitting. One said, "Hey, John, what are you doing here?" So I addressed them all: "Pop quiz: Who here knows I'm dating Tom?" One guy raised his hand. I went on, "Well, now you all know, and knowing is half the battle." I smirked and walked back to Tom's room. I knew that everything would be just fine.

Sigma Nu has become my home—a stable place at a school whose quarter system makes stability hard to come by. I have been elected Eminent Commander (what we call our president) for the summer term. It's an honor I carry with me wherever I go, and my brothers are honored to have me as their leader. No one can pledge until his sophomore year at Dartmouth, but I feel blessed for having had that first year with Tom and with the other Sigma Nu seniors who left before I could officially join.

I believe that if you are closeted in a fraternity where being gay is not acceptable, you have two options: One, stay closeted and waste a few years of your emotional life. Two, come out and try to change the place you're in to a more gay-friendly space. Whether you find acceptance will tell you whether you should leave the house or stay. Anyone who reacts negatively to your newfound homosexuality is not a friend and never was.

I'm so much more confident and comfortable with my sexuality because I'm allowed to exercise it here, around people I love, people I interact with every day, people who are my close friends. Tom and I did eventually break up, but I can still bring boys to our formals. I can dance with them at our dance parties. I can give my boyfriend a kiss in the TV room when he comes to visit. That's something I don't think I would be able to do if I lived in a dorm, and something that is more special because it's not an issue. I mean, honestly, you can't really get more acceptance than when you bring someone home to your room and your suitemate waves at you both as you walk in the door and says, "Have fun guys." ★

Lessons in Sharing
by April Whirley

This year our chapter visited The Methodist Home for Children and Youth for Easter. The children share the cottage they live in with seven other kids. We arrived on a Saturday morning and went to each of their cottages to hide eggs.

I was overwhelmed with everyone I met there—the volunteers, the faculty, and especially the children themselves. There was one cottage I am often reminded of when I think of the unity we yearn for as brothers and sisters in Greek life. The cottage was home for eight boys between the ages of seven and thirteen. Much like fraternities and sororities, they weren't related, but by living together they acted like each other's family.

The boys were filled with excitement when we opened the doors and let them run wild looking for the eggs. Most ran around finding eggs with no problem, looking for the next egg as they picked up the first. But Josh ran slower than the rest and he was one of the last to get through the door. I could see disappointment in his expression, and every time I tried to point out an egg I remembered hiding, someone else would grab it up just before my little friend. When the hunt was over, Josh only had one egg.

After the boys made one last sweep to make sure the eggs were all gone, they started eating the candy. One ate almost his whole bag before he even glanced up to see what was happening next. I could hear two of my sisters warning others that their tummy was going to hurt if they ate any more. It was so much fun to watch the boys get all excited, but my attention remained on Josh as he watched everyone else laughing and eating.

I wasn't the only one watching Josh. I noticed several of the other little boys glance his way. I kept thinking about how I should have left a few eggs out in case something like this happened. Looking back, I am glad I didn't have any extra candy, because I would have never seen this profound lesson in sharing.

A few minutes passed before one of the boys walked across the room and handed Josh a piece of candy, then one by one they all followed. To see the boys give up their candy and their "three o'clock snack" doesn't seem like a big deal, but that candy was all they had to share.

I stood back and couldn't help but wonder. "What if my sisters would do that for me?" So often I hear people talk about the time and money they don't have. If that candy could represent the time, money, and effort that go into our sorority, then everyone has something and we all have a lot to give one another. ★

The Legacy Of Brotherhood
by Dale Davenport

Roger and I were roommates during our sophomore year, forging a friendship in the heat of our fraternity pledging semester that we thought would last a lifetime.

There were double dates, weekends at each other's homes, summer trips to the shore. Our birthdays were just two weeks apart, and in our senior autumn, newly 21, we spent many a Friday afternoon elbow to elbow down at the 'Skeller.But graduation was always just around the corner. And when it came time for ours, Roger headed off to Dartmouth for an MBA, and I, after a short stint with The Associated Press, had a national obligation to fulfill. I recall a letter or two during Officers Candidate School or while I was in Vietnam, but we soon lost touch. The last I heard, Roger was working in Hong Kong.

All the memories came exploding back last week with the news from Kansas City. Roger, a vice president in charge of Pfizer Inc.'s Kansas City operation, was gunned down in a parking garage at the airport. Police say the killer was hired by the former boyfriend of a woman Roger was dating. The couple had just returned from a weekend in New York and were loading their luggage in his car when Roger 's life came to an abrupt end.

It was a life that, sadly, I knew little about. Suddenly, I found myself wanting to fill in the blanks between the days when we shared Rolling Rocks and dreams of the future and a 90-second spot on "America's Most Wanted" about the man who paid to have him blown away.

A few phone calls yielded clips from The Kansas City Star and biographical data from Pfizer. That eased my curiosity. But grief remained, grief not so much for a man I no longer knew, but for a friendship that once seemed so durable and that proved so very vulnerable, and for a part of my life that now is gone. The longer the journey of life, the more finite and defined are our relationships. In youth, we think our friends will always be with us. As time passes, it becomes increasingly clear that these are just episodes, pieces of a much larger puzzle that we spend a lifetime putting together.

And as the puzzle goes together, our perspective changes. When Roger and I met, our goal was to get through pledging in one piece and enjoy the weekends. Only later would we begin to refocus on planning for a job or, in his case, graduate school. We knew or hoped that much of our lives lay ahead, but it was all pretty fuzzy
because it really was just a dream.

At 20, our future is that big expanse of life past age 25. At 30, perhaps we can see 40. Only in middle age does one begin to look 25 years down the road, to retirement and beyond.

So, too, in middle age do the events occur more frequently that cause us to look backward.

In the last several days I've thought a lot about the good times we had, Roger and me. Our college years were everything that everyone had told us they would be. We found our spouses-to-be and built a foundation for successful careers.

Roger 's, I discovered last week, took him through the Far East. At one time, he was Pfizer's youngest "country manager," responsible for sales of pharmaceutical, agricultural and chemical products in Hong Kong and Macao. After stops in Sri Lanka and Taiwan, he came back to the states in 1981 and worked his way up the corporate ladder.

I settled in the 'Burg and began a long relationship with The Patriot-News. For whatever reason, each of us decided to lead his own life, content to let our friendship rest as just one of those episodes. People come and go in your life, you hope that they enrich it, but there is always a time to move on. We moved on.

But I can't help wondering if Roger found fulfillment. He obviously was successful, but according to the newspaper he was going through a divorce. He and Diane had two daughters. They must have been devastated by this horrible crime.

Roger also lost touch with our other close college friends. He must have found new ones. Pfizer's president issued a statement calling Roger a "friend and colleague" and "a vibrant and talented member of the Pfizer organization, whose leadership and enthusiasm touched us all." Perhaps his work became the central focus of his life.

These are just musings, of course, for the episode involving Roger and me ended long ago. My life has been rich and full, and I've got memories of other friends, other times and places, that make me smile.

Still, some memories were just his and mine. Everyone has them for the people they touch, and that's why, when they go, a little part of us goes, too.

Over the years, a little part of me missed Roger. I can't fix that, but there are others whom I miss, others I remembered as the shock of Roger's death began to subside. I really ought to work on fixing some of those relationships while there's still time. Call it an old friend's legacy. ★

Inspiration for Greeks

Decision of a Lifetime
by Ellen Dunseth

Bid day at Iowa State University is always filled with fun and excitement. The prospective members, Rho Chi's, and chapter members, gather on the central campus near the Campanile. During my second year of graduate school, I served as the Panhellenic council advisor. The week of formal sorority recruitment was ending and I was emotionally and physically drained. I was looking forward to returning home for a long, relaxing weekend.

The Bid Day activities began. Music was playing. Photographs were being taken. The women were laughing and chanting their favorite sorority songs. The Rho Chi's gathered in the front with their recruitment groups, while the chapter members anxiously waited behind. The Rho Chi's distributed the sealed envelopes to the women in their groups. For many of the women, the next few months would completely change their lives. For one, Jennifer, it did just that.

Jennifer had transferred to Iowa State that fall. During recruitment, she became very close with Liz, another woman in her recruitment group. Liz and Jennifer hit it off from the beginning and secretly hoped they would join the same chapter. When the two women ripped open their bid cards and realized they wouldn't become sorority sisters, the panic set in.

As I watched the prospective members open their cards, hug each other, and then scatter off to join their new sisters, I noticed the two women in the middle of the crowd. Jennifer was crying uncontrollably and Liz was trying to comfort her. The Rho Chi motioned for me to help. I ran over to see what was happening. My first instinct was to move to the side so these two women weren't standing in the middle for everyone to notice. As we began to talk, I realized Jennifer hadn't received her first choice. They had attended the same preference parties and both desperately wanted to be members of the same chapter. Unfortunately, Liz had been extended an invitation to join this chapter, and Jennifer had not.

Jennifer, Liz, and I snuck away from the crowd and settled in my office. Luckily, another Greek affiliated woman, Laura, who worked in my office, was around to help with the counseling. By this time, Liz and Jennifer were both crying. Liz asked me if she could give her invitation to Jennifer because she really wanted it more than she did. At that point, I almost lost it. The two women talked about their recruitment experience and how they had become good friends and now wanted to be sorority sisters. Laura continued to talk with Jennifer, while Liz and I went out into the hall. She confessed to me that she still wanted to be in this particular chapter, but felt bad for Jennifer. We decided that we would walk over to the chapter and see if she wanted to stay for their bid day activities. Liz was welcomed the moment we arrived, and when I left she was smiling.

I returned to our student union where I found Jennifer and Laura still talking. We talked for about four hours. Jennifer shared with us that she had a boyfriend and was a little homesick. She talked about her relationship with her parents and her need to succeed. In some ways, Jennifer wanted the best in everything that she did and not being invited to join her first choice was a failure in her eyes. Eventually, we contacted the president of the chapter that had given her the invitation. Nikki, the chapter president, was amazing. She ran over as soon as we told her that Jennifer was a little apprehensive. Nikki listened to things that might not be very easy to hear. She comforted a woman who didn't really want to be her sister. We found out that Jennifer didn't really like her current living quarters on campus and Nikki offered to let her move into the chapter house if she wanted. Nikki was a true sorority woman.

A few hours later, and many Kleenexes used, Laura and I walked Jennifer back to her residence hall room. On the way back we convinced Jennifer to go by the chapter house that night or just give Nikki a call. She said that she would. We left not knowing what would happen to Jennifer of if she would join the chapter she had been invited to. She seemed more content, but still very confused and disheartened.

It wasn't until the ncxt semester when I saw Jennifer again. I had heard Jennifer did move into the chapter house and was very happy. I chose not to contact Jennifer because I assumed she wanted to just forget the experience. We were beginning a recruitment round table when I looked over and saw that Jennifer was sitting next to Nikki. She introduced herself as the assistant recruitment chair. It was sort of ironic that Jennifer, the prospective member who didn't get her first choice, found the silver lining in her new home and now wanted to share that with other students.

During Greek Week, I saw this young woman glow once again as she participated in Lip Sync with her sisters and fraternity men. It was a captivating experience to watch her smile, as I recalled the tears from only a few months ago. It truly made me proud of her.

I haven't spoken with Jennifer since bid day, but I hope she realizes how much I have learned from her. I hope Jennifer realizes how special her experience has been at Iowa State. Many women are offered an invitation to join their first choice and never appreciate that gift. Through Jennifer's experience, I have learned the value of appreciating my Greek affiliation and realizing the pride in being Greek. I have come to realize that a sorority isn't the letters on the house or the crest on the wall. It is the women whom you form friendships with and memories you make. It is the happiness you feel during ritual and the pride you show during recruitment. By chance I joined my organization, but it was love, friendship, and support that encouraged me to stay. Thank you, Jennifer! ★

Fraternity: A Decision and A Commitment
by Paul M. Buckley

I remember vividly the tense air amid forty-plus men in a room too large for timidity and too small for false pride. I had been invited to "the smoker"—an opportunity to get to know the fraternity brothers more intimately.

Earlier that evening I had carefully ironed my shirt and slacks, inspected my blazer for lint, and gone to the barber for a fresh haircut. I needed to look impressive, sharp. Two days before, I had scurried off to the mall from my last class of the day to purchase a new tie for this most important occasion. And here it was at last.

Be cool, Paul. Be cool, I told myself and glanced at the envelope in my hand to confirm it was still there. This was my ticket. In that envelope was an essay—typed, double-spaced, and without grammatical or spelling error. I followed the directions I had been given to the letter. All I needed to do now was to hand it over and remain cool and confident.

With over forty prospective candidates in the room, I could feel the energy of a silent competitive spirit in our presence. The reality was the Fraternity would not be inducting a line of forty new members. I surveyed the room, taking note that no one else had on my tie. I only hoped I could show these fraternity men my unique qualities and somehow find myself set apart from the rest. The tie didn't really matter, but it was something that made me feel better. It was something I could see. I wouldn't know what the other candidates expressed in their essays. And I had no clue what their grades were. As for character and leadership, I could only guess what some of my competitor's resumes looked like and I didn't really know who these men were. I could only concentrate on me.

When the fraternity brothers officially started the program, they encouraged all of us to relax and be ourselves. The tension decreased, but not significantly. There was little anyone could do about that. Even as we talked and laughed, I knew this could possibly be one of the greatest decisions I would make in my life: to pledge this historically Black fraternity. The brothers emphasized to all of us that evening that although fraternity life seemed like all fun and play from the outside looking in, it was much more than that. In reality it was a challenge to have a little bit of fun while working to be true to a lifetime commitment.

Later that evening, after I had returned quietly to my residence hall, I closed and locked my room door to have some privacy. That night I began a three-month-long decision-making process of whether or not to pursue membership in the fraternity. I made a list of advantages, such as leadership, networking for change, and strong sense of comradeship. I also made a list of my perceived disadvantages, which included a loss of individuality. As the weeks and months progressed, I read articles and books that had any reference to fraternal organizations and secret societies. I investigated the fraternity's history more deeply than had initially garnered my interest, and read in awe the achievements of its prominent members. I thought carefully … a lifetime commitment.

Nine years later, I am still an active member of the fraternity that has given me a sense of cultural responsibility, an extended family, and the rewarding experience of service. The decision I made is one I would make over and over again and just as carefully because it has changed my life in powerful ways. It did not take long for me to learn that image is nothing without achievement and leadership. So today I am even more careful to prepare for success, and allow excellence to show its own image.

Sometimes I pick up my old journal and reread the list I made on that night so long ago. My understated advantages were so limited, yet they still outweigh my perceived disadvantages. The fraternity has been a catalyst for positive and inspiring relationships within the organization and interfraternally as well; the training I've received has made me a confident contributor to society at large; and my quality of life in the human experience has been impacted profoundly. I am still a unique individual, but I now understand my connection to and interdependence with others. Fraternity is not about who I am, but the unity in diversity that makes us who we are. ★

Butterflies in My Sky
by Nicole Carnes Shipley

"What time do you want to leave for the game?" asked Julie. It was never a question of if we were going somewhere together, but when. Julie and I became friends instantly when we met on bid night. We had a common interest in having fun without drinking alcohol. We would walk to all the Purdue football games on gorgeous, sunny afternoons. We used to dance all around our big sorority house just laughing. Most nights, we'd see each other in the bathroom while getting ready for bed. I am a messy tooth brusher, so Julie would always have a paper towel ready for me when I needed one. Then we would trudge up the big cement stairwell to the cold air dorm. We picked our beds so they'd be next to each other. Julie and I would make faces at each other, trying not to laugh out loud and wake the others. I remember lying in my cold air bed and feeling the cool breeze blow across me from the window as I drifted off to sleep.

During one night in the fall of our junior year, Julie and I did our sober duty together at a function. We pigged out on cookies, made up silly dances, and laughed all night. We were oblivious to the party going on in the next room. "Smile!" our friend Anne prompted as she took a picture of Julie and me.

The next morning, Julie asked me to turn in an application for her on campus. Julie was going to be at the airport all morning since she was a pilot. She handed me the application with a yellow Post-It that read, "Love ya Nic, Jules." We hurried out the front door to leave for classes. "Bye, Julie!" I said smiling. "Bye, Nic!" she answered. Julie was wearing her golden hair down that day, and it glistened as the warm sun shown down on it. She drove away, with sunglasses on and shimmering hair blowing in the warm breeze.

That was the last time I saw Julie. Hours later I found out that her plane had crashed.

Our whole sorority drove down for the funeral on a bus. There was a special feeling of togetherness. The day was sunny with a majestic blue sky. We all stood together, arms around one another, in front of Julie's grave. We sang our special sisterhood songs and weeped. As I walked back to get on the bus, I stopped for a moment and stood in the wavering green grass. My long, flowered dress waved in the breeze. Up above me, against the blue sky, were thousands of butterflies. Butterflies are one of our chapter's beloved symbols.

After the funeral, we were all invited over to Julie's house. A group of us enjoyed the beautiful weather out on the deck. As we reminisced, a butterfly came and landed on a branch right next to my arm. This butterfly stayed on the branch, slowly fluttering it's graceful wings, seeming to listen in on our conversation. I couldn't help but smile.

There have been many times since then that I have seen butterflies in strange places, and I know that others have, too. A butterfly circled and swooped playfully around me and another pledge sister as we walked home from class one day. Another time, I was driving on the interstate, missing the company of my dear friend. I looked out my window and saw a butterfly gliding alongside my car. I thought it was odd that a butterfly could keep up at that speed.

Exactly one year after Julie's death, I was on a retreat. When it was time to have a quiet time, I wandered out into the woods and sat on a log beside a rippling creek. I opened my Bible, and pulled out a picture taken of Julie and me the night before she died. Deeply missing my friend, a butterfly came and landed on my Bible. It sat with me until I was no longer sad, then it flew off into the wind. ★

Inspiration for Greeks

What I Thought About My Greek Advisor During ...
by Anthony J. D'Angelo

Summer Orientation:
What the hell do I care what this guy has to say? I'm Italian, not Greek.
Welcome Back Week:
Oh, I get it! He's the guy in charge of fraternities.
My First Semester:
Those frat guys are cool. I wonder if they like that guy?
Second Semester Rush:
He seems to be a really nice guy. At least he gives a good speech.
Pledging:
The brothers here tell me, "Watch Out! That guy is an jackass."
(Even though they've never met him personally.)
Induction Week:
Wow, it's pretty cool how that guy sent me a congratulations card.
(I should meet him someday.)
1st Semester as a Brother:
Yeah! That guy IS an jackass.
(Even though I've never met him personally.)
My 1st Inter-Greek Meeting:
Oh, "that guy" has a name. That guy is Charlie.
My 5th Inter-Greek Meeting:
Boy, Charlie really seems to care about us. It's 10:30 p.m. and he's still here.
My 7th Inter-Greek Meeting:
Hi, Charlie, my name is Tony. It is nice to meet you.

The Summer of My 2nd Year:

Oh Hi, Charlie. I didn't know that you work during the summer too. I thought you got your summers off, just like the faculty.

The Fall of My 3rd Year:

Really Charlie! You think I should run for Vice President?

Chapter Vice-Presidency:

Charlie, these guys just don't seem to understand me. They think WE don't like them. I could really use your help. What do you think I should do ...?

The Fall of My 4th Year:

Charlie, would you mind meeting some of our new recruits. I would really like to give them the opportunity to meet you. After all I talk about you all the time.

The Spring of My 4th Year:

Charlie, I can't believe it is coming to an end. (Oh, could you write a letter of recommendation for me?)

Graduation Day:

You'll never understand how much of an impact you've had on me. Thank you Charlie!

Years Later:

I wonder how Charlie would have handled this? That guy sure knows a lot. Man, I miss him. ★

Beyond The Black Pants
by Megan Wilson

When I first came to college, I had this vivid picture of what the Greek system must be like: frat guys with beer bellies, cheesy pick-up lines, and low GPAs drooling over girls wearing black pants, pounds of makeup, and fake smiles. I had heard stories about college frat parties. I saw Animal House, and I figured that I had better things to do with my time and my money. To me it was all just a superficial circus. I only owned one pair of black pants anyhow.

This was, of course, before I met the sisters of Zeta Tau Alpha. I attended a membership recruitment meeting (to provide moral support for a friend, not of my own free will), and I remember looking around the room hoping to prove my prejudices correct. Much to my surprise, not one member was wearing the standardized sorority black pants, and I don't think there was an ounce of mascara in the room. I actually enjoyed meeting these girls, and I figured there was a small chance that sororities might not be as bad as I had thought. So, after much deliberation, I decided to become a new member. My mother made an appointment with my doctor to have my head checked.

I have to admit that my new member period not only dashed all my previous negative impressions of sorority life, but began building toward the most positive experience I would encounter during my college years. All of a sudden I was surrounded by strangers who would become my friends, and then my sisters. I didn't think it was possible to find good friends in seventy-five people, but I found a place among them, and security within them. I found friendships I knew would last a lifetime, and a sisterhood I was proud to be a part of. I've always hated being wrong, but I was willing to eat my words this time.

My mother always said it's hard to tell how strong a friendship is until it's tested. The bond I had with my sisters was certainly strong, but I didn't know how strong until it went through the ultimate test. I needed them because of Brandon.

I met Brandon the summer before I started college. I went to Florida for a week with my best friends from high school, and Brandon was staying at our hotel. I thought he was a cool guy from the start, and he made the trip as memorable as it was. As much fun as I had with him, though, I didn't realize at the time how much of an impact he'd have on my life.

At the end of the week he went back to Cleveland, and I to New York, and soon after I left for college in Baltimore. I talked to Brandon every night without fail, and we got a chance to see each other a few times. It's strange how people can get under your skin so quickly, but he did, and I might be the only one who will ever understand that. It doesn't seem enough to say that he was my best friend. Brandon and I were so much more. People like that only come along once in a lifetime, and when they do, we need to take everything they are and tuck it way down deep inside us so we can keep it forever. People like Brandon change us, and I'm a better person because of what he was to me.

I was lost when he died in September of my junior year. Nothing ever prepares you for things like that. I felt like a part of me died, too, and I didn't know how to go on without it. I didn't feel like I had anyone to turn to, because it seemed like no one understood. After all, I had only seen him a few times since I had met him, and I guess that doesn't constitute a relationship in the eyes of most people. But I felt an emptiness inside me that couldn't have been put there by someone who was just passing through my life. I still feel that emptiness, and I always will.

Understandably, my schoolwork suffered, as did my social life. I didn't know how to reach out to anyone, and it was hard letting anyone in. Death has such a numbing effect, and it kills something so pure and beautiful inside those left behind. I didn't laugh for a long time. I didn't cry either. I just waited for him to come back, and when he didn't I fell apart. My sisters were there to pick up the pieces.

I must have received about twenty-five phone calls the night I found out about Brandon's accident. I don't remember what was said as the night was a blur, but I remember hearing the voice of a different one of my sisters every time I picked up the phone. At our first meeting after I returned from the funeral, my sisters were waiting with hugs, cards, and comforting words. They gave me all their support without even thinking about it, and their kindness kept me strong through the hardest time in my life.

I think that's when I realized what a sorority was all about. It wasn't about black pants, parties, and frat guys. It was about something deeper than friendship. It was a family. It was about pulling together when a sister was hurting, and not giving up until the hurt went away. It was about never letting anyone feel like they're alone. I know now that all my sisters have felt alone at one time or another. I think that's why we all came together in the first place.

Brandon used to make fun of me because I joined a sorority. I think now he's glad I did. In fact, I wouldn't be surprised if he had a hand in sending me the seventy-five angels that helped me get my life back. ★

True Brotherhood
by Mark Jacobsen

In the summer of 1999, my brother, Scott, committed suicide while I was away at school. Being near the end of term and right before our much-needed long weekend, the news really hit me when I needed it least. Unfortunately, Kettering University is six hours away from my hometown of Greenfield, Wisconsin, but my co-op employer chartered the president's private jet to bring my uncle out to get me at our chapter house. I'll never forget returning home to an entirely darkened house and my entire family, friends, and neighbors. My Mom just sobbing on the steps is the saddest thing I've ever witnessed.

The next three days were the worst I've ever had. You just can't imagine the amount of sadness and sorrow until you lose someone you are close to.

But the one thing I can never forget happened as the processional into the church was about to begin. As the other pallbearers and I got into line, walking up the sidewalk came ten of my brothers from Phi Gamma Delta. I couldn't help but shed a few tears. Not only had they skipped classes, exams, quizzes, and the beginning of a long weekend to be with me, but they did it with less than a day's notice and with a six-hour drive to a state that most of them had never been in. Because of their unselfish love and support, I was able to get through giving the eulogy and the next few days. It was on that day that I truly appreciated the fact that while I had lost my one brother, I still had more brothers than anyone could imagine. ★

The Tattoo
by Marquerite Murer

Taking a deep breath, I stared at the ceiling. As a Tri Delta Field Consultant, I already had three successful rush visits under my belt, but this one was going to be different. My coordinator, Julie, had made it clear this was not going to be easy. In fact, it was going to be near impossible. I didn't need to look at the file again since I had almost memorized the statistics. Our Utah chapter had been steadily declining for years. We were far below chapter total and had not made quota during rush in over a decade. The chapter had to constantly open rush during the year and there was plenty of fighting among the members. They were bright girls, involved on campus, and had good grades. A few were really wild according to some of the members, and presented an image problem. But the biggest problem was that the chapter took members of all religions, which our Fraternity strongly supported. That is a good thing across the nation, except when your chapter happens to be in Salt Lake City.

The Mormon faith is so strong and powerful in the area. I had been briefed that all of the strongest sororities on campus only took Mormon women. While our chapter had some Mormon women, it was not a deciding factor during rush. Julie had carefully explained that my role was to give these women hope and inspiration. She stressed that my charismatic personality was the main reason for my assignment to Utah. The executive board wanted these women to believe in themselves and each other. They knew the past statistics and issues on campus had the odds incredibly stacked against them, but they believed we could improve our rush results.

There was a knock on the door as Jody, the chapter president, peeked her head into my room. She asked if I was ready and I thought to myself, "Get out the pompons and markers."

Walking into the filled dining room, I was greeted with curious looks. After introducing myself, I explained that I would be participating like the rest of them in the pre-rush workshop. As the rush chair, Megan, began talking about the skits, I noticed the senior crew. Of course, they were in the back of the room at the very corner table and were muttering under their breath. As I watched one-too-many eye rolls, I went over to sit with them. This had little effect. An argument erupted over how rotation was going to work. Two members walked in late, and the assistant rush chair said they were each fined ten dollars, which caused another fight. Megan tried to regain control of the room by telling everyone how important this rush was for the future of the chapter. One of the smart-aleck seniors yelled out that it didn't matter anyway, because "Nationals" was just going to close the chapter. She finished her declaration by staring at me. Standing up, I enthusiastically explained that Tri Delta did believe in the chapter and that I was there to help them. I agreed with what Megan had been saying and encouraged her to go on. Skeptical eyes turned from me back to Megan. The afternoon turned into evening without much change in the atmosphere or much productivity in rush preparation.

After the chapter had been dismissed, I gathered the glum rush committee. I asked for three impressions from the afternoon. Megan let out a frustrated sigh and said she felt like we got nothing done except fight. Jody was worried that it seemed like many of the members did not even care. Karen was concerned that we wouldn't be ready with our skits, songs, and rotation. Questioning eyes turned to me as I looked at tomorrow's schedule. With a twinkle in my eye, I asked if there was a park nearby. Jody said yes, only a few blocks away. Grinning, I said, "Okay, this is what we are going to do."

The next morning, Karen and Jody were nowhere in sight as Megan took roll call. Once that was complete, she told the chapter to leave everything in the dining room and follow her. The seniors immediately started grumbling, so I told them this was not optional. Following Megan outside, people asked where we were going. She just smiled and marched on. I brought up the rear of the group and refused to say anything. The sparking sun and cornflower-blue sky had people smiling as they walked across campus.

As the chapter crossed the street to the park, Karen and Jody greeted everyone. Picnic tables were covered with pop-filled ice chests, Rice Krispy treats, and hotdog supplies. As I gathered everyone around our makeshift campfire, I explained that today we were going to do something really important. We were going to focus on each other and remember why we pledged Tri Delta in the first place.

Of course, a senior snorted, which I ignored. I went on to explain that we were going to play, laugh, and just be silly. Later on we would tie things into rush, but first I wanted to see them laugh together. Though hesitant, I could see that some of the younger members thought this was a good idea. We started off with a lively game of frozen tag, then moved into my special version of Red Rover. When a team called someone over, they had to add on why they wanted that person. Watching from the sideline, I laughed as Kristy was called over because she is a good basketball player. Becky was called over because she can cook, while Kelly was called over because she is smart. By the time Red Rover was over, everyone was laughing.

The morning passed quickly as we played red light/green light and Tri Delta charades. As everyone munched on roasted hotdogs and chips, I told them to look around and think about why Tri Delta is important to them. I asked them to focus on simple things, like laughing together, giving someone a hug, and cheering someone on. Passing around bags of marshmallows, I asked them to each say one reason Tri Delta was important to them. Leaning back against a pine tree, I smiled as the various answers were shared. "I always have someone to study with." "There is always someone willing to listen to my boy troubles." "I can always find someone to go running with me." "I know that when I have a bad day, someone will make me laugh." "When I have a great day there is always someone to share it with." "I have become a better leader." "I have found friends that are different than me and that helps me grow." On and on the answers went. As I watched them all smile at each other, I knew we had found what was important. Now we could move forward.

Climbing onto a picnic table, I quietly explained that you have to believe in yourself, each other, and your goal. I reminded them that the pine tree is a symbol of our Fraternity. It has deep roots to withstand turbulent times and it always points hopefully upward. I continued on that rush is really about letting people see who you are and what Tri Delta has to offer. I explained that at yesterday's meeting, I did not know who the chapter was, what they were about, or even if they liked each other. Today, I knew they genuinely cared about each other and believed in the chapter. If they could just focus on enjoying each other over the next few weeks and celebrating their sisterhood, it would shine through during rush. Then rushees would want to be a part of their special sisterhood.

I wrapped up my heartfelt lecture by explaining that it was important to set a goal and create an incentive for when the goal was reached. The incentive would inspire the members when they were doubtful and would help them stay focused. For example, we could have a pizza party when we increased the number of rushees pledged. Or we could have another picnic at the park. Members quickly caught on and started shouting out suggestions. We could all go hiking in the mountains. We could have a special dinner at the house. We could all get tattoos. Suddenly many others chimed in that tattoos would be so cool, since it was the fall of 1991 and the tattoo craze was just getting started.

As more and more members declared they would get tattoos on their ankles, my mind flashed back to my thick files of statistics. Fall of '90 quota was thirty-five and the chapter took seventeen rushees, fall of '89 quota was twenty-seven and the chapter took twelve, and so on the stats went. Logically, there was no possible way the chapter would make quota, which was set for thirty rushees per chapter. I finally agreed that if we made quota, we would get tattoos. As deeply as I wanted them to believe in the impossible, I just prayed that we would do better than seventeen rushees from the year before.

The next several days raced by as member's spirits soared. Rotation practice was often interrupted with jokes and songs. Skit practices were awesome and members laughed at every opportunity. They were becoming confident in themselves and their chapter.

Two days before rush was to start, a fight broke out during a rush procedures discussion. Cynthia and Kim argued back and forth about references. Trying to referee, I asked them to calm down. Of course, the senior back table decided that was a good time to add some comments. It was if the air was let out of a balloon. Sassily, Missy said, "This all probably is for nothing anyway. Who are we kidding? We can't change the way things are done on this campus."

"That is it," I quickly interrupted. "We are going to wrap things up right now for the evening. Tonight I want you all to really think about what you want out of this rush. Then I want you to think about the past few days. Watching you all grow close and embrace your sisterhood is not nothing. No matter what happens in the next few days, you already have succeeded since you have found each other again."

As the members quietly left the room, I once again gathered the rush team. After a few quick questions, we agreed to meet back in the dining room at midnight.

Sipping a diet coke the next morning, I carefully watched the member's faces as they came down the stairs. Eyes popped open as they slowly moved from the living room to the family room and finally to the dining room. Bright colors splashed every inch of the walls. Quotes from our Founders, our past presidents, and other influential leaders cheered us on. Sisters began to call out favorite sayings to each other and shoulders seemed to become more square. Jeanette wanted to know how long it took to make all of the posters. The rush team just smiled. Holly laughed and asked, "Do you all really believe in us?" We all nodded yes. I winked at the rush team and stood up. With a long look, taking in every single member, I firmly

said, "We are not giving up. We are going to succeed."
The final days passed with confidence and adrenaline.

The energy in the chapter was electrifying on the morning
of first round parties. Decked in matching fuchsia Tri Delta
tee-shirts and khaki shorts, the members were ready for rush.
As the clapping thundered throughout the house, I prayed that
everything would be okay. Confident smiles and enthusiastic
chatter filled each round of parties. More than once I heard a
rushee say that it seemed like the Tri Deltas were having so
much fun.

That evening we gathered for our meeting, and the room
seemed to explode with pride and joy. Smiling, I congratulated
them on an awesome first round. Sobering a little, I reminded
them that tomorrow would be a challenging day. They needed
to be prepared that many rushees would drop Tri Delta simply
because the chapter encouraged diversity. They must, though,
continue to portray the confidence and enthusiasm that flowed
through the parties today.

Night passed to day, and we found ourselves lining the
halls waiting for the second day rushees. I confidently high-
fived members as they began their cheers. With brave smiles
they were out to show the rushees why Tri Delta was so special.
As the last rushee was ushered in the house, I prayed that all
would go well. I was proud of the strength the women had
showed earlier when I announced that forty-seven percent of
the women we had invited back had accepted. They knew they
had a tough battle ahead. As I carefully climbed around rushees
and Tri Deltas, I couldn't help but smile as I heard members
talking about how much fun they have together. I heard snip-
pets of stories of playing Red Rover, of decorating the chapter

house with inspirational signs, and the quiet comfortableness of being around people who genuinely care about each other.

The rest of the week was a blur of songs, Under the Sea skits, lemonade, and pep talks. Though our pool of potential rushees was slim, the members passionately believed they would make quota. When spirits sagged, songs would break out while others began to draw marker tattoos on their ankles. I just smiled and hoped.

As we gathered for our final meeting after preference parties, the members seemed to radiate joy. Exhausted, they collapsed onto the floor, many leaning on each other. I asked each of them to share what they were most proud of during rush. Some boldly called out, "We rock as dancers!" while others said, "We are all so close to each other." Yet another said, "We were really organized and prepared." Someone else whispered, "We believe in each other and Tri Delta." The silly and the serious comments seemed to light the room with a special goal. Finally, sparkling eyes turned back to me. Wiping the tears from my own eyes, I shared that I was so proud of them. That no matter what happened the next day, they already were a smashing success because they believed in Tri Delta, each other, and most importantly, themselves.

The next day the Delta Delta Delta chapter at the University of Utah proved that the impossible could happen when they pledged thirty-two women, which is quota plus two. I've got the tattoo to prove it. ★

The Conference Call
by Kim Littlefield Dowd

I had the extreme pleasure of traveling as a field consultant for Delta Delta Delta the year after I graduated from college. I was one of six consultants who traveled around the U.S. and Canada to various colleges and universities where DDD had chapters assisting chapters in assessing their strengths and needs, meeting the officers, alumnae and campus representatives, and facilitating leadership development programs. The six of us—Cheryl, Cynthia, Jeanette, Meg, Michelle, and I—met in June at our national leadership school for field consultant training. We spent a total of about ten days together over the course of that summer before hitting the road in early August. Each of us was at that time (and still is) very different, but we had two significant things in common: membership in Delta Delta Delta and experiences as "road runners" for DDD.

We became fast friends! Each of us made a point of writing and calling one another as often as we could. Because we traveled independently, we spent very little time together. But that didn't keep us from developing strong friendships. A job as a field consultant is unlike any other, and unless you've done it before it is hard to relate to the experience. Understandably, when we got left standing at the airport with no one to pick us up, or had the most fantastic day seeing a new part of the world we had never before seen, we naturally turned to one another to share our thoughts. This was before the advent of email and toll-free voicemail. Boy, did we ring up a huge phone bill!

Early in the spring of that year, our supervisors, Cari and Julie—who we affectionately called our FC Moms—notified us that we were going to have a group conference call to discuss some issues. Once we were able to get eight varied schedules synchronized for the call, we were all on the line. "Hi, everyone! How are you? How is everything going? What are you doing for your next break?" The questions and laughter were endless. With eight women and one phone call, it was hard to get a word in edgewise.

After the opening chitchat, Cari and Julie jumped right into the issues. Number one on the list was that here it was only February and we were close to expending our budget that was to last through June. And guess where we happened to be overspending the most? Yes, the phone bill. Big surprise! The six FC's sat quietly on their ends of the line and silently and respectfully resolved to find other ways to stay connected with one another. "Of course, girls, we want you to feel supported and connected to one another. We have great team spirit and we want to maintain it," Julie said, "But we have to find a way to cut back on our phone expenditures." Each of us chimed in, "We understand." After a few more minutes of some more pleasantries, everyone wished one another well and began to sign off. One by one, each of us gave salutations to our friends and Moms. Someone suggested that we all hang up on the count of three. "One … two … three", we heard, and in unison we all said "Goodbye!"

After a few moments, the six FC's realized that we had all stayed on the line … that is, all but our supervisors. We had no prior plan to stay on the line, it just kind of happened that way. Once we realized we were all still on the line, it was like six pairs of eyes lit up. We felt we had hit a jackpot! We stayed on the line another twenty minutes before the operator and our FC Mom, Julie, broke in an said in a sing-song voice, "Ladies, what are you doing?"

There was stunned silence. We knew we had been busted. The silence slowly faded into laughter. Once the laughter subsided, Julie said, "OK, we're hanging up now, right?" We dutifully responded in chorus, "Right", then echoed Julie's "Goodbye". As I went to hang up, of course I listened to see if any of my FC friends stayed on the line. We weren't lucky enough to get away with it twice!

We finished our year of traveling, and have many wonderful experiences and memories to show for it. I also have seven special friends who are still an important part of my life despite living in various areas of the country. It is still amazing to me how quickly we became friends even though we did not have the opportunity to spend a lot of time together. I now know that sisterhood and lifetime membership are not necessarily just about seeing one another every day. Incredible bonds can be developed and maintained through the small ways we are present in one another's lives. ★

Everything Happens For A Reason
by Michael Andreano

I always wondered what fraternity life would be like. I was curious what it is actually about. My gut feeling was that it wasn't for me. I wasn't a big beer drinker and didn't see myself going through campus on panty raids, singing songs, or other typical fraternity related activities. I began college that fall with a very "it's not for me mentality". The school itself was a small private engineering college. Certainly there were no "Animal Houses" on this campus. They'd all fail out! Even with this in mind, I was still not sold on the idea of going Greek.

Orientation began that Tuesday. As I went through some of the introduction seminars to get better acquainted with college life, little did I know that some of the people I would meet within the first few weeks at school would impact me significantly and get me to where I am today.

Once I finished moving all of my things into my dorm room, I headed to the main building and met my group leader, the person we reported to each day to begin orientation. The group leader introduced himself as Anthony. He was a junior, a mechanical engineering major, and currently active on the Greek council. "Oh, no!" I thought, "already I met a frat guy." He seemed like a good guy though. Pretty straightforward, easygoing, liked sports, and pretty social. He couldn't say which fraternity he was from. The rush rules for orientation stated that no one involved with the freshmen could wear their letters, fraternity clothing, or verbally reveal their chapter name. I got to know Anthony that week, when inquiring about books for classes, he had made a deal with me to sell his calculus, chemistry, and physics books to me for a cool seventy-five dollars. This was a steal, as each book had practically cost that much just on its own. I wish I knew which house he was from at that point. I really wanted to check it out.

During that same week I met George and Roy. They were two of my team leaders for the team building activities during the orientation week. They were very different. George was a bit more my kind of guy. He was clean cut, kind of preppy, medium build, and pretty social. Roy was a bit skinnier, wore a hat, smoked cigarettes, seemed a bit less outgoing, and liked classic rock. Regardless of their differences, both were very good team leaders and helps us all out explaining, demonstrating, and helping us with each activity. Once again, both were Greek, but could not say which house they were from. After meeting those three Greeks, I started becoming more open to what Greek life may have to offer. I figured they were all from different houses, since they all seemed a bit different.

Greek rush began that first Monday of school. Seemingly out of nowhere, Greek letters, posters, and schmoozing began all over campus. I hadn't seen George, Roy, or Anthony the first few days that week. I began my work-study job in the admissions office. The student who I was reporting to was Eddie. Eddie was kind of funny when I first met him. He talked really fast and liked to laugh. Right away I enjoyed working with Eddie. He was wearing his fraternity letters on this yellow sports jersey with the name "Fast Eddie" on the back. I talked to him about what he thought about Greek life. He said he was really happy about joining his house and told me how he was hesitant at first but went through rush and then found a house that fit him the best and decided to give it a try. He encouraged me to do the same. I asked him what his letters were—

not knowing the Greek alphabet yet. Well, the X was called Chi, and the O with the line through it was Phi. Pretty neat, I thought, at least now I knew two of the letters.

Later that night, many of the houses did "dorm storming" on the freshman dormitories. Each house had two members going door-to-door, knocking on each and introducing themselves to you and giving you their two-minute commercial about what makes their house so great. (This gets old quick! Having ten houses doing this three or four times a week makes you really want to leave your room between 6 and 8 p.m. each night.)

After a few houses came by, the brothers from Chi Phi stopped by. They introduced themselves as Billy and Vic. These guys seemed a lot different than Eddie was. Since my room was the first on the floor, when they went to write down my name they realized they had not brought a pen. I let them borrow one which they returned later (come on guys, get with it). I had told them how I met Eddie up in admissions. They told me some more about the house, the size of it, the costs, the meal plans, and some of the history.

They invited me down to their house for a casino night later that week. They also handed me some flyers. Casino Night, huh? That seems cool, I thought. I told them, "Count me in." When Thursday arrived, I went down to Chi Phi. When I walked in, I got my $500 of Chi Phi money and headed up to the Blackjack tables (the only game I really knew how to play at the time). Low and behold, there was George. I said hi to him. He mentioned how he was looking for me during this week but we kept missing each other. He showed me around a bit. I also bumped into Eddie. He shook my hand

and welcomed me as well. I then saw Anthony and Roy over at the roulette tables. At that moment I was really spoofed. Could all the people I happened to meet in my first week or so have come from the same house? It certainly appeared that way.

As rush progressed, I did check out the other houses. Unfortunately (or fortunately—depending on how you look at it), no other house really fit me as well. I felt most comfortable at Chi Phi. When I received my bid, and then pledge night got closer, I did some thinking. Was it really a coincidence that I happened to meet so many different people, all of whom were a bit different, but yet I hit it off with each of them in their own way, but yet they all happen to be from the same fraternity and share that common bond of brotherhood? When I thought about it, I knew that going Greek was really a strong possibility and that Chi Phi would be that house.

It was four years later that I became president of Chi Phi. Freshmen whom I rushed several years ago are going to graduate this coming month. In two months, I will be attending my third national leadership conference as an alumni volunteer leader. I still ask myself when I look back on my college years. Was it a coincidence that I met the Chi Phi's that I did, when I did, and that I ended up pledging there and becoming a brother? I think not. Everything happens for a reason is what many people tell me. My response? It certainly does. ★

Virgin Sisters
by Aja Kosanke

I started pledging for a sorority my freshman year of college. It was pretty scary at first. I didn't know anyone that well that I was pledging with. I liked them all very much, but no bonds had been made yet. I felt like everyone was good friends with at least one of the others. I found myself sitting alone. I wanted to talk to these girls. They all seemed really great. They were girls I would handpick for my friends. The only problem is, I felt like I had nothing to say.

One night at our weekly meeting, we were all doing an activity together. It was a "get to know your sister" thing. We were all trying to think of things to ask. Of course, being the way we were made them all kind of funny. I think we had a disability for being serious. Anyway, one of the girls said we should all say when we lost our virginity. I was frozen. There was nothing to be ashamed about, I know that. I never met anyone I felt that deeply about yet. I mean, I'm not made of stone or anything. There were some definite close calls. However, I could never go through with it. It wasn't a problem to me, only, it's not one of those things you could blurt out easily. I mean, an 18-year-old virgin is kind of pathetic. Anyway, someone said that we shouldn't just In case anyone hasn't had sex yet. I calmed down for a minute, until everyone said that they had. What was I going to do, lie?

I was going to tell them. Okay, this is great. One of my most private secrets was about to be revealed. When someone asked me, I thoughtlessly blurted out, "um, 17." Alright, it was over. No harm done. This is my private business, and it was all okay. Until I heard someone say, "I'm a virgin." I don't think I was ever so surprised, relieved, and guilty at the same time. I wasn't the only one. Even friends of mine that were still in high school have all had sex. I haven't had anyone to relate to since I was a junior in high school. I suddenly didn't feel so alone.

I thought about it the entire week. Why didn't I just admit it? Was sex that big of a deal? Now this poor girl felt like she was the only one. Meanwhile, I took the easy way out. Later on I found myself hanging out with this girl all day. We just kind of hit it off and had a lot of fun. It was weird, because I almost forgot that she was a virgin. I was planning to say something to her, but it didn't come to my mind until the end of the day. All of a sudden I just blurted it out. I was actually screaming it and laughing at the same time. That's how it was with her. We would just laugh about everything together. We both started jumping up and down, and gave each other a big hug.

That was it. I had made my first of many bonds. We became such great friends. It's weird how it started. Virginity, it's so not a big deal. I now realize there was a reason for someone to suggest such a silly question. A question I feared for so long brought me a friend who I know and will be in my heart for a lifetime. It was then I realized that friendships can't be forced. They sneak up on you when you least expect it. The point is we are never alone. There is always someone we can connect to in some way or another. I feel like the luckiest girl in the world. I now have over sixty sisters, and I love them all. I will never be ashamed of who I am again. Everyone should love each other for who they are. After all, that is what sisterhood is all about. ★

Never Alone
submission by Bob Mead Colegrove

I was a student at SUNY Fredonia from 1987 to 1991. Coming to college was a scary time for me because I was a middle child. Most people that are a middle child have an older sibling to look up to and ask questions. When I was fifteen, my older brother, Lee, died from a gun accident. He was playing around with a gun and it went off. There was a bullet in the chamber.

So I went to college with no advice from my brother, Tommy. My freshman year I joined the Sigma Phi Epsilon fraternity. Understand that at SUNY Fredonia we are not a large Greek school. Our chapter has about forty members. I did not take on a big leadership role in the chapter because I became an RA and did my part by recruiting several members each semester.

My goal was to help my little brother, Lee, who was still in high school. Whenever he had problems in school, I would talk to him on the phone for hours. Girl trouble, I was there. I felt as though I was helping him as much as I could. One Saturday, during my senior year, my parents were supposed to come up and see me and Lee was supposed to come. He had gone to a friend's house the night before and was still tired. I tried to convince him to come up and see me, but he said he was really tired. That day I had a great time with my parents. They left early that evening and I went over to a brother's house to hang out.

I got a phone call from my cousin. She told me to get back to the halls ASAP. We started fighting on the phone because I didn't know why I had to come back right away. She finally told me, "We have to get you home." The five-minute ride home from the brother's house was the longest I have ever had to endure. When my cousin got me into the car, my aunt, uncle, and cousin told me that my younger brother, Lee, had died—a suicide.

My life was over. I was alone. I didn't know who to turn to. My family was all together for the week. At the wake, I sat in the back and just cried. I was now an only child.

I looked up and in came fifteen of my Sig-Ep brothers. They drove two hours to come and see me at the wake. Each one gave me a hug and told me they would make sure everything at school would be taken care of. They stayed about an hour-and-a-half, then drove back to Fredonia. My fraternity believes in giving of your time and talents for the chapter. That day I saw my brothers give of their time for me.

Why is this story so important to me? I don't feel alone anymore. I went on to graduate school. (I almost did not go back after that week.) I got married and after several years away from Fredonia, I was hired to work as the Assistant Director of the student union at Fredonia. My old chapter counselor was getting more responsibilities put on his job at the college and needed to step down. The chapter needed someone to give of their time and talents to take his place. Those were very big shoes to fill, but I said I would. Now, I have forty undergrad brothers that need me as much as I need them, a great job, and a wonderful wife. ★

Inspiration for Greeks

The True Bond
by Jenel Guidry

It was a normal day in the routine of our exhausting lives, all except for, well, what was wearing on some of our minds. We had to decorate the place just perfect in enough time so that we could spend an equal amount of time on our own décor. It was Date Party, an event we plan for weeks to insure three hours of fun-filled excitement with your sisters and, of course, the perfect date. This year's theme was camouflage … "You can run, but you can't hide from a Sigma Tri." Many of us were hiding from something that stirred much deeper within us than face paint and a cute pair of camouflage overalls.

It had been a year since our last date party, only last year's theme was "Woodstock". It proved to be a night of peace, love, and harmony with our sisters and brothers. Together, bonded as Greeks, we supported one another through the loss of a member of Kappa Alpha Order earlier that morning. May 1, 1999 was a day that the Greeks of Southeastern Louisiana University would never forget. Date Party meant something else that night. It meant a gathering not for special purposes, but for us to join in our time of sorrow. None of my sisters were left alone that night to ponder life's most difficult questions. Although we could not supply answers, together we would conquer the often considered option of being alone. This young man had taken his life; however, we would never be able to let go of the memories. I remember how horrible it felt—the initial pang in my stomach and the tears that hid my incomprehensible eyes. I could not help thinking of his family … his brothers.

So here we were a year later, planning what used to be a traditional Date Party. Everything was set. The place looked like a scene from the movie *Saving Private Ryan*. There was camouflage everywhere, only I was not bringing Matt Damon. My date and I were really good friends, but he was not who I would usually bring to such an event, which was a bit strange at first.

The night was going great. As president, I worked the door as usual then mingled among the crowd. Everyone was having a blast. It was my last Date Party, and it was going to be memorable. Near the end of the evening, after various snapshots and the typical huddle to the song *We Are Family*, I was named Sweetheart of my chapter. I would never forget this night!

While dancing with our new Beau, the DJ announced that I had a phone call. The voice on the other end was muffled by tears, yet familiar in tone. It was one of my sisters who was out of town. She continued to ask me if I could hear her or if I could go outside. My heart dropped. I initially froze in dismay, but soon melted in tears. It could not be true! Not now, not ever. As the music came to an end, so did my impression on life. From that moment my thoughts would never be the same. As the chapter and their guests gathered to hear the closing speech, which was also traditional, I searched for the strength to describe a night that would never be traditional again! It was the hardest moment of my presidency.

Somehow, I had to tell my members that one of our sisters had died earlier that morning in New York, while on a trip for fashion merchandising. April 15, 2000 is a night we will definitely never forget! Once again, together we consoled one another and searched for impossible answers. The only thing that seemed remotely clear was that we are sisters forever, "Faithful Unto Death." My date, being a member of the Kappa Alpha Order, assured me that once again, together we could endure. Strange as it was to be there together, it all started to make sense; he had already experienced such a loss.

The cause of her death is still unknown due to inconclusive autopsy reports. However, the reason for her life is easier to explain. She touched so many lives in her short period of time. A lesson we all learned from her was the meaning of giving. After sending flowers to my mom, who was extremely sick in the hospital, she told her mom of her good deed but would not say what she had done. She explained that if she did not take credit for her deed or brag about it, it would be returned to her twofold. Unfortunately, the florist put her name on the envelope, I knew. I never told her.

At dinner a couple of days before she left, I told her I wanted to go with her to New York. I explained how she could leave me there to enjoy a new city with new potential and atmosphere. She responded with an explanation of how there was no way she could stay there because she had too much to do here, and I must stay for my chapter and to complete everything I had started. It hurts that I am still here and she never returned.

At her wake, as she laid before us in our colors, we placed her badge over her heart. I know that is where I will always keep the memory of her. Suddenly, the terms "sisterhood" and "ritual" had a new meaning. Whoever said Greeks are mischievous or negative influences, because they are often bashed by the media, obviously never experienced such a bond of true sisterhood and brotherhood. Without my fellow Greeks, I could not have survived these experiences. ★

The Homecoming
by T.J. Sullivan

In high school, I was one of those kids lucky to find a date for the Homecoming Dance. But four years later, things were different. I was different. I had been selected—along with four other "big men on campus"—for the Indiana University Homecoming Court. I was riding high.

For those of us who majored in extracurricular activities in college, being selected to the Homecoming Court was the equivalent of graduating with honors. Each year, a committee of powerful, well-groomed students would solicit applications from the most active leaders on campus, conduct unnecessarily intense interviews, grade, rate, and select.

The final selections were usually predictable: student body president, interfraternity council president, a student who had an amazing community service record, and at least one student of color. Throw in a standout member of the "Singing Hoosiers," a student athlete, a handful of sorority and fraternity presidents, and your formula was complete.

The brightest, shiniest students trotted out to midfield during the football game to assure alumni that Indiana was still producing strong contributions to the Midwestern gene pool. These were the students who were chosen first at the business school interview meat markets. These were the students who had the right resume, the right connections, the right image, the right looks. Honestly, the people typically chosen for Homecoming king and queen hardly needed the self-esteem boost. They were already winners.

So, what the hell was I doing on the Homecoming Court?

I was definitely a well-connected student leader. I had done a little of everything: reported for the student newspaper, served in the residence life student association, served on the interfraternity council (in a low-level capacity), and had been a founding father of my fraternity chapter of Pi Kappa Phi. I had served on quite a few random, meaningless university committees. The university president knew my name, and the student body president was a good friend and a regular drinking buddy.

But I had some serious negative marks against me. During college, I worked at least two jobs at all times, forty hours per week, putting myself through school on out-of-state tuition. My grade point average was a whopping 2.7. I was not much of a presence in the student leadership party circuit. While most of the homecoming candidates were running off to date parties and barn dances, I was flipping pizzas at Noble Roman's.

My fraternity felt it was important that someone applied each year, and sadly I looked like our best hope. Next thing I knew, I was borrowing a suit from a fraternity brother, heading off for an interview I was sure would be humiliating. I was not looking forward to justifying my college career to the well-groomed student committee.

My attitude changed, of course, when the announcement came that I was selected for the court. My fraternity chapter was positively ecstatic. Other fraternities and sororities began running advertisements in the student newspaper congratulating me. It was an obvious public relations move by the Greek community, but it felt really good to see my name in 24-point type. My coworkers at the pizza joint harassed me mercilessly and made me wear a paper crown from Burger King during my shift.

I knew I was the mutt of the litter, but the attention I gained from being named to the Court was fantastic. We, the chosen ones, were invited to receptions hosted by the alumni association (I had to borrow a second suit). Professors smiled at me in the hallways of the journalism building. I got congratulation notes from former lovers.

By the time the weekend before Homecoming arrived, my ego was in overdrive and I was milking the experience for all it was worth. I finally broke down and used one of those student Visa cards to buy my first suit. I wanted to look acceptable during those five minutes I would stand on the artificial turf at Memorial Stadium.

Then, on Tuesday of Homecoming Week, with festivities at full tilt, the phone call came from my father. My grandfather had suddenly died at age 87, and everyone back home in Maryland was in complete shock. The funeral was planned for Saturday, and the ticket would be waiting for me at the airport Thursday evening. I was expected home.

I had been incredibly close to my grandfather, and the news was devastating. In many ways he had been one of my very best friends.

My emotional high from the Homecoming activities had made the phone call even more bizarre. My mind searched for a way to do both things I needed to do. The timing was horrible. My grandfather had died during the most incredible week of my life. Years of putting myself through school and making a contribution to my campus had culminated in this one particular Saturday. And I would be spending it in my new suit, in a funeral home in Southern Maryland.

To make matters more unbelievable, I received a short letter from my grandfather the next day. He had written and mailed it the day before he died. He wrote about his flower beds, still blooming in mid-October. He wrote about the weather. He talked about his bowling league (he was still playing at age 87). He wrote about how he wasn't "feeling so hot" that day and how he hoped he would see me soon.

Up until that moment, I had been actively avoiding the foregone conclusion. I would be missing the Homecoming game and my moment in the sun. Self-pity and grief had been battling inside my mind. But now, I didn't care as much about the Homecoming. My friend was dead and I needed to be home for my family.

I called the powerful, well-groomed committee. To put it mildly, they were extremely unhappy about my need to miss the event. The young woman who was the designated "candidate liaison" even went so far as to ask if my family could reschedule the funeral for Sunday. "I'm sure there's a flight to Maryland after half-time that would get you there in time."

My fraternity brothers, Kevin and Jason, called me that Saturday evening. They had announced my name at the game along with the nine others (I had thought they wouldn't), and a great guy who was a member of Phi Kappa Psi fraternity had been named king. I had been announced as the first runner-up.

We all face those times when a choice has to be made between something you want to do and something you need to do. Homecoming was one of mine. Even when you do the right thing, you are left with an unavoidable sense of regret.

Would the outcome of the Homecoming king contest been different if I had been there? Maybe. I'll never know, and I don't much care anymore. I don't remember the name of the guy who won the contest and I don't remember the score of the game.

Today, I still have the letter my grandfather wrote and the paper crown from Burger King that my coworkers made me wear. I remember how good it felt to feel rewarded. I remember how ugly that first suit was. And I laugh when I think of my grandfather.

I think he spent that day at the football game. ★

Sorority Girl
by Kristina Ferrick

Ten years ago, I would have never seen myself as a "sorority girl". But, that was then …

When I was three years old, I met a young girl in pre-kindergarten school. Her name was Wendy, and she became my best friend in the whole world. When I was ten, my father's job took us from our New Jersey home to Florida, and I left Wendy behind. Over the years we became closer, even though the distance still physically separated us. I would go to New Jersey for a visit and she would come down to Florida to stay with my family and me. There was no friendship that was ever stronger than ours.

When we were eighteen, she was visiting from New Jersey and we decided to go out to a show. Unfortunately, at the same time, a man and his friend decided to leave a bar and get behind the wheel of his truck to go home. They hit us head on, and Wendy was killed instantly. After many weeks in the hospital, I was allowed to go home and try to put my shattered life back into order.

I returned to school, a sophomore in college, the following January. I was lost and so alone. I happened to run into an old friend in the cafeteria and he was telling me about his upcoming fraternity rush. He was excited because it looked like it was going to be a great year for his fraternity. They had so many potential pledges and so many great things planned. That's when I asked him the question that changed my life. "What makes being part of a Greek organization so exciting?" That's when he introduced me to Debi.

Debi was a member of a local sorority that had just gone

through the major change of becoming the newest chapter of a larger national sorority, Theta Phi Alpha. This, of course, meant nothing to me; neither did the letters on her shirt or what they stood for. These were all things I thought I'd never understand.

Debi spoke to me for about twenty minutes, then invited me out with her and the other members of Theta Phi Alpha for their first spring rush event. I told her I didn't think I could because I did not have a car. I explained that I lived almost an hour away, my car had been totaled in the car accident, and that I had to carpool with my father just to get to school. I also told her I was scared to drive that far at night because I was still shaken up about what had happened not four months before. Debi then said something to me I will never forget. "I'll come get you. I think it's important that you meet every-one." So I went, and I met most of the founding sisters of the Beta Nu chapter of Theta Phi Alpha. I had a great time.

I pledged Theta Phi Alpha that spring, but it was tough. I had to try to concentrate on my schoolwork, learn the history of Theta Phi Alpha, and deal with the loss of my friend. The first two I did on my own, but the last was the hardest and most difficult. The hole in my heart that Wendy's absence left was so big and so empty that I felt I would never overcome it. I found the strength I was lacking in my new sisters. Even though I had only known them a short time, they went out of their way to help me with the grieving process. Listening to me when I needed to talk, being a shoulder to lean on when I needed to cry, and holding me when I thought there was just no end to the pain. They did not try to take her place or try to get me to forget her. They just softened her absence with smiles and filled the void with love. That's when I discovered the deeper meaning behind the letters we all wore on our shirts. They stood for caring, understanding, and unconditional love and acceptance. It did not matter that I was new to the organization. What mattered to them was I was in pain and they did all they could to make sure I was not alone.

It's been almost ten years now since I became a "sorority girl". Debi is my big sister in our chapter. Hope became my friend and confidant, and Becky became my role model. I am now a conference director for our national organization and I am still involved as an alumna for our local chapter. Many sisters have come and gone throughout the years, but one thing remains the same. When I get the "I'm missing Wendy" feelings, I simply have to make a phone call and I have someone who will listen if I want to reminisce or weep if I don't feel like crying alone. I couldn't ask for more than that.

It's funny—ten years ago, I couldn't see myself as part of a sorority. Ten years from now, I can't see myself without it. ★

Touching Shoulders
by Tammy Rembert

In my junior year of college I wanted to associate myself with a sorority. It would become another first to add to my life—(a) first in my immediate family to graduate from a four-year university, (b) the first person at Grambling State University to pursue a double major in marketing and mass communications, and (c) the first in my family to become a part of a black Greek organization.

Since my exposure to black Greek organizations was non-existent, my choice of which sorority I would become affiliated with would be based on what I wanted and not who, rather be it family or friends, already belonged to them. All four sororities were in active status on campus and because it was the fall semester, interest meetings were on a rampage. I had friends in all of these sororities, so I knew the general information about each one of them. At first I decided to attend all the interest meetings to get a feel for what each sorority was about, its members, involvement in the community, and the expectations for membership.

However, something happened that changed that plan. My mother was diagnosed with breast cancer. At that point I was ready to quit school and go home to look after my mother. Being the strong woman she had always been, my mother assured me that everything would be alright and I needed to stay and complete my education.

With that said, I continued my education and got back on track. However, by this time most of the interest meetings had already taken place, and so I figured I would join a sorority in my senior year. Then one day while walking in the student union, I saw a flyer for an interest meeting and I decided to attend. The event was very professionally done, both the undergraduate and the graduate chapter members were very personal with the crowd. They greeted everyone as they walked in the door and they answered questions in a positive manner. One could tell that these ladies were proud of their organization. Toward the end of the program a member stood up and faced the audience. She began reciting this poem:

Touching Shoulders
There's a comforting thought at the close of the day,
When I'm weary and lonely and sad;
That sort of grips hold of my poor old heart
And bids it be merry and glad.
It gets in my being and it drives out the blues;
And finally thrills through and through.
It's just a sweet memory that chants the refrain;
"I'm glad I touched shoulders with you!"

Did you know you were brave?
Did you know you were strong?
Did you know there was one leaning hand?
Did you know that I waited and listened and prayed
And was cheered by our simplest word?
Did you know that I longed for that smile on your face,
For the sound of your voice ringing true?
Did you know I grew stronger and better because

I had merely touched shoulders with you?
I'm glad that I live, that I battle and strive
For the place that I know I must fill;
I'm thankful for sorrows; I'll meet with a grin
What fortune may send, good or ill.
I may not have wealth, I may not be great,
But I know I shall always be true;
For I have in my life that courage you gave
When once I rubbed shoulders with you.

When she was finished, I had tears in my eyes and I knew I had found the sorority for me. You see, it was this same poem that my mother had sent to me after she had completed her treatments. God truly works in mysterious ways and He had sent me this divine intervention that I was not going to ignore.

On February 7, 1991, I became an exquisite member of Zeta Phi Beta Sorority, Inc. In May of 1992 my mother saw me walk across the stage receiving both of my degrees. She met many of my new sisters and was quite impressed with their demeanor, their outlook on life, and most of all their strong faith in God. She, too, agreed with my decision.

In December of 1992, six months later, my mother was called home. I was never alone during this tribulation in my life because my Zeta sisters were there "answering the call". So you see, I was destined to become a Zeta woman. The final attribute that confirmed my decision was the fact that those Zeta women were willing to touch shoulders with me. ★

A Letter to Home
by Anthony J. D'Angelo

Dear Mom and Dad:

Since I left for college, I have been remiss in writing and I am sorry for my thoughtlessness in not writing to you sooner. I will bring you up to date now, but before you read on, please sit down. You are not to read any further unless you are sitting down, okay?

Well, then, I am getting along pretty well now. I have recently been initiated into the best fraternity here on campus. But the skull fracture and the concussion I got when I jumped out of the window of my dormitory when it caught fire shortly after my arrival to campus is pretty well healed now. I only spent three weeks in the hospital and now I can see almost normally and only get those pounding migraines once a day.

While in the hospital, I met a wonderful nurse who stood by my bedside 24/7. She is a lovely woman named Bonnie, who is recently divorced with three boys of her own and a little one on the way. As a matter of fact, I think you may know her. She graduated from State the same year you guys did. Upon my release from the hospital, Bonnie was kind enough to take me in since I had nowhere to live due to the dormitory fire.

Bonnie was kind enough to invite me in to live with her and her three boys in their "apartment". It's really a basement room in her ex-husband's girlfriend's ex-husband's rental unit. (I know this sounds confusing, but when you meet them you will understand.)

With me on the mend and Bonnie on the rebound, she could not resist my charm. Within weeks we fell deeply and passionately in love and are planning to elope in Tahiti. We haven't got the exact date yet, but it will be before Bonnie begins to show.

Yes, Mom and Dad, you are going to be grandparents! I know how much you are looking forward to this and I know you will welcome the baby and give it the same love and devotion and tender care you gave me when I was a child. The reason for the delay in our marriage is that I have a minor infection which prevents us from passing our pre-marital blood tests, and I carelessly caught it from Bonnie's ex-husband's girlfriend.

Now that I have brought you up to date, I want to tell you that there was no dormitory fire, I did not have a skull fracture, I was not in the hospital, I am not eloping, there is no woman named Bonnie, and you're not going to be grandparents. However, I did join a fraternity and I want you to see my decision in its proper perspective. Besides, the guys here are really, really cool and it means a lot to me to have new friends like the ones I have now. I've told them all about you and they look forward to meeting my cool parents this semester!

Your loving and devoted son, Tony

P.S. Dues are $350 per semester. Please make check payable to Theta Chi Fraternity. ★

A Knight to Remember
by MariAnn Callais

I have been a Greek advisor for the past nine years, and through those years I have seen celebrations and sorrows and growth in many of my students.

One summer, I learned a great deal about brotherhood and sisterhood and what being a Greek community was really about. That summer seemed to be like any other. Many of the students had gone home for the summer and a few had stayed to go to summer school. I was going through the normal motions of planning for the fall and getting everyone ready for summer orientations.

There was a student I had met when he was a beginning freshman. His name is Marvin. He was quiet and yet there was something about him that just made you like him. Soon after being on campus, he pledged Kappa Alpha Order and began getting involved. He asked if he could work in my office and I said yes, thinking this would be a positive experience for him. He became an orientation leader, got involved in the fraternity, and was doing exceptionally well in school.

The next year things began to change. Myself and others noticed he drank a great deal, seemed to not really care about himself, and we noticed a great change in his behavior—especially his grades. Here was a student who was on the Dean's List now doing so poorly that it was obvious something was not right.

Marvin was becoming very troubled. Every time anyone including myself would confront him, he would give this funny little smile and say, "MAC (that's me), don't worry, it's all good". I don't know if he knew it or not, but many people really cared about him and were really concerned.

Toward the end of the spring semester, Marvin and his girlfriend were having problems. He came to visit me out of the blue one day. I said, "Marv, what's up with Al?". He said, "She's taking a vacation, but it's all good". He said she was tired of putting up with his bull. He called one time after that visit, but I would never speak to him after that day.

I saw Al and she told me basically the same thing as Marvin had said. They were taking time apart and who knows what would happen.

About two weeks later, I was home visiting my family and I received a call from my friend Kelly. It was 3:35 a.m. My dad woke me and said, "Kelly is on the phone." I knew right then that something was wrong. I said hello, and he said that Marvin had taken his life. I said I could not believe it and I was on my way."

The series of events that happened were very painful, and yet very much an example of why Greek life is so important.

The students were all devastated. We had not had this kind of tragedy hit our Greek community before. There were so many tears and so much pain and hurt. None of us could believe it. In those three or four days I learned what true brotherhood and sisterhood is all about. I learned that no matter what letters you wear on your chest, or how much you may dislike another group, during a time of need everyone becomes a Greek family.

I was angry at Marvin and sometimes I still am. But I know that through the tragedy of his death, it has taught many of us to appreciate the opportunity that we have to be Greek.

His KA brothers raised money to give Marvin the last gift they could give him. That gift was a headstone for his resting place. On that headstone is a picture of the Kappa Alpha Crest. When you give someone something even after they have left this world and you continue being there for them, that to me is a true example of living our ritual and being the brothers and sisters our founders must have wanted us to be.

Marvin is a Knight we will always remember. ★

What Every Member Needs to Know
by Robert J. Kerr

New member education is always a paradox. How do we transmit the appropriate knowledge and information without giving away membership to anyone who can afford the dues? A dilemma which has puzzled me, and I suspect every chapter, alumnus, and Greek advisor in North America, for some time. So I decided to sit down and create a list of things I wish I had known when I was a pledge.

1. The purpose of your fraternity/sorority.
2. The values of your fraternity/sorority.
3. Which actives are committed to living items 1 and 2.
4. How to chair a chapter committee.
5. How to work with alumni/alumnae.
6. The history of your organization, both national and local.
7. Who your personal role models are and why
8. How to successfully recruit.
9. Respect is a gift we all must earn.
10. How to properly use the Greek Advisors office.
11. How to lead an event that satisfied risk management needs.
12. How to speak in public.
13. What the 7 rules of writing are, and how to use them.
14. How to resolve conflict without shouting or using violence.
15. How to confront members not meeting obligations.
16. That it is up to you to make the chapter stronger.
17. How to facilitate positive change in your life and chapter.
18. The tradition of the ritual is our only genuine tradition.

19. Everyone/everything can be improved with time and love.

20. Love is what fraternity/sorority genuinely means.

21. The chapter needs you more than you need the chapter.

22. Who to talk to at your headquarters and communicate with them at least once before initiation. Even if it is just to say thank you.

23. All pre-initiation activity should be of a reflective nature. There is no need for fear/intimidation/physical activity or sleep deprivation.

24. Membership is a journey, not a destination. The real work starts after initiation.

25. There is no such status as junior active or any other form of secondary status. Once initiated, you are entitled to full and immediate privileges. Call headquarters if anyone says differently.

26. There are actives who are not good members. Learn who they are and avoid them.

27. If you consume an alcoholic beverage and are underage at a chapter event, you are risking the life of your chapter.

28. Always know how to find the centers of influence in a group.

29. Learn how to discover the fear that is the underlying source of most anger and hatred.

30. Learn how to disapprove of a person's behavior and not the person.

31. Uncover your special gift, nurture it, and then share it.

32. Bylaws never override: a) state law, b) university policy, c) ritual, d) common sense and reason.

33. Your primary job is to find people better than you and get them into your chapter.

34. Always treat people with love and respect.

35. Remember, your duty is to defend the ideals and principles of the fraternity/sorority. Not the members who violate the ideals and principles.

36. If alumni come by the house to drink and tell war stories, learn how to ask them for help with your career over a cup of coffee.

37. Never trust anything you hear once someone has had a drink of alcohol or mind-altering substance.

38. Meet the university president.

39. How to use proper table etiquette.

40. How to find joy in giving/helping others. ★

Crossing Over
by Ana Martinez

A bookmark in my mind I remember the day,
The unforgettable day when I saw the light.
I now march along those who paved the way
And uphold a sisterhood so worth the fight.
No matter what I will always voice my love
My love for it and my pride for it.
Every single thing I now do
Has a much deeper meaning to me!
I am a lady
And strive for the very best.
Through times of struggle I put myself to the test.
My inner strengths have been unleashed!
A sisterhood nourished by cultures so rich,
Such diversity, yet we are all held together.
Letters, simply letters, to others they may be,
But to me they are engraved in my soul forever.
I was taught to accept the things I cannot change,
However change the things I truly cannot accept.
I am a sister of Lambda Theta Alpha
I exude unity, love, and respect! ★

How I See My Chapter
by Raul Marquez

Today I see my chapter dig a hole and plant a tree in it
Today I see my chapter open the door for a lady
Today I see my chapter talk about ritual and what it means
Today I see my chapter relive memories about I-week
  and initiation
Today I see my chapter raise awareness about
Violence and abuse against women
Today I see my chapter pass out white ribbons
Today I see my chapter build a party
Today I see my chapter help a church
Today I see my chapter invite a brother to meeting
Today I see my chapter being great
Tomorrow I see my chapter being even greater. ★

The Meaning of Home Sweet Home To A 22 Year Old Fraternity Man
by Mark Walker

Bzzzzzzzzzzzzzzzzzzzzzzzzzzzzzzzzzzzzzzzzzzzzzzzzzzzzzz. The sweet smell of sweat lingered over me as the round, squishy belly of the tattoo artist rubbed against my thigh. The pain seemed like a thousand wasps swarming the room that decided only to sting my ankle and the ankle of my friend. No, my brother. I was lying down on the form fitting recliner looking off to my right. Jeremy lay there, blanked faced and looking at the ceiling.

On the wall to my left was the face of Jim Morrison in a drunken stupor with a series of numbers under his picture. His eyes were deep black circles. It was as if his mind were not in the room with the prison guard and photographer. I remember thinking to myself, lying in that chair, that it would be cool to have a mug shot. It would be cool to go to jail for having a good time at the expense of the law. But my mind was not in that room…….

My mind was thinking of myself at fifty, walking up to the steps of Jeremy's house. I hadn't seen him in years. He opened the door and his eyes widened as he invited me in. Before one of us could speak, I lifted my pant leg to reveal that while my leg hair had become gray and sparse, the letters Kappa Sigma still shone as bright as they did the day we walked out of the tattoo shop.

We favored our bandaged ankles and talked of friendship, brotherhood, and the next girl Jeremy was planning to hook-up with. We were young, and the ink that was forever soaked into our ankles spoke more sincerely about our friend ship than any nineteen-year-old boys ever could. ****************************

Brotherhood never meant much to me before I drove up to Tallahassee. It meant no more to me than a word I could not define. I remember sitting at home with my Florida State acceptance letter clung to my palm watching the news with my parents.

The story of the night, like always, was negative. A freshman at the University of Florida died that evening. He fell off the rood of his fraternity house during a party. His life was over that night as I clung to my acceptance letter like a trophy.

My mother, like most mothers, imagined that boy was her son. As she pictured in her mind me, falling off that strange roof, in that strange town. She said that fraternities were nothing more than lonely boys looking for other lonely boys to cling to.

I help onto that acceptance letter and like my first cigarette I told her that I would find out for myself. ************

Four years latter, as I returned home for my final Winter Break, I sat with my little brother in our parent's living room.

He asked me why I joined a fraternity and why I had decided to label my ankle with letters that were foreign to him. I was silent for a moment. And before I spoke I crossed my leg and fingered the letters on my ankle. I rubbed over the skin, outlining the letters that were red and bordered by black. Feeling the hairs that jutted through my pores and out through the colors. "You wouldn't understand," I said with a hint of pride.

What I meant to say to my brother was that while he and I shared the same blood he was not my only brother. What I meant to tell him was about the warmth that I felt when I walked into my fraternity house. It is like the feeling that you get when you come home from school and walk into your parent's house to see your mother talking on the phone. Or feeding the dogs. Or cooking your favorite home cooked meal. Home Sweet Home.

What I wanted to tell him is that I get that same feeling of warmth when I walk into my fraternity house. Warmth is the feeling that I get when I walk into my house to see Todd sitting on the couch playing Nintendo. Warmth is the feeling I get when I see my brothers helping each other. Warmth is the feeling I get when I come home and see Nick drinking a beer and dancing with himself in the corner. Home Sweet Home.

This may sound funny or odd, but think of it as a blanket that you've always had. Much like a child is invincible when he puts on his imaginary force field simply by hiding under the covers.

I live with my friends. I don't live in an apartment, a dorm room or a rental house. I live in a beer soaked, cigarette smelling, broken glass covered, overflowing trashcan filled, fraternity house. And I would not trade it for anything. I live with my friends. I live with my brothers. For me this is my new Home Sweet Home.

WOULD YOU LIKE TO SEE YOUR STORY IN INSPIRATION FOR GREEKS™ VOLUME II?

All of the stories that you have read in this book were submitted by readers who are Fraternity Men, Sorority Women and Greek Life Professionals like you. We would love to have you contribute a story, poem, quote or cartoon to:

Inspiration for Greeks™ Volume II

Even though we are planning to launch several other Inspiration Books over the next few years, (see inside front cover for details) we are always looking for more Greek Stories to create Volume II.

Feel free to send us stories you write yourself. It also could be a favorite poem, quotation, cartoon or story you have seen that speaks to your Greek Experience. Just make sure to send as much information about you and the source of your submission.

Please send your submissions to:
The Collegiate EmPowerment Company, Inc.
The Inspiration Book Series™ Submission Department
PO Box 702 Lambertville, NJ 08530
Or Fax It To: 609.397.0833
Email It To: Inspiration@Collegiate-EmPowerment.com

If your submission is accepted & approved your message will touch the lives of thousands of Greeks across the country!
(Of course you'll get a free book too!)

An Overview Of
The Collegiate EmPowerment Company, Inc.

The Collegiate EmPowerment Company, Inc.

"The Leader in EmPowerment Education for Today's College Students"

The Collegiate EmPowerment Company is a nationally recognized educational firm dedicated to empowering college students & student affairs professionals with the most interactive, inspiring and informative empowerment seminars & products.

We are the only organization in the world solely dedicated to serving college students & student affairs professionals. Since 1995 we have served over 1 million students & clients from over 1000 colleges across North America, The United Kingdom & Australia.

In addition to the Inspiration Book Series™ We serve college students & student affairs professional like you with the following tools & resources:

"Young Adults EmPowering Young Adults"

EmPower X! is the instructional team of The Collegiate EmPowerment Company. EmPower X! is an elite kick ass team of young & professional adults, all under the age of 30, who facilitate the What College Forgets To Teach You® Seminars. Each member of EmPower X! is a Certified Collegiate EmPowerment Coach™, who has been hand selected & personally trained by Anthony J. D'Angelo.

What College Forgets to Teach You® The cornerstone of the Collegiate EmPowerment Company is its What College Forgets To Teach You® Seminar Series. A curriculum series of over 30 comprehensive & integrated seminars, created by Anthony D'Angelo, exclusively designed to address the challenges typical of most college students & university graduates. The series consists of four different levels of seminars, each containing distinct concepts, tools, strategies and systems. Each seminar reinforces the others and deepens a student's understanding of his or her own vision & purpose in life.

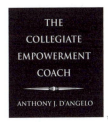

THE COLLEGIATE EMPOWERMENT COACH

ANTHONY J. D'ANGELO ™

The man who is Helping You Take Higher Education Deeper™ & the Founder of The Collegiate EmPowerment Company, Anthony J. D'Angelo. He has been hailed by CNNfn as, "The Personal Development Guru Of His Generation" and SPIN Magazine has compared D'Angelo with the likes of world renowned peak performance expert, Anthony Robbins.

Today Anthony serves as the Chief Visionary Officer of The CEC & is the creator of The Inspiration Book Series and the architect of EmPower X!. He is also the #1 Contributing Author and Editor of The New York Times Bestseller, Chicken Soup For The College Soul. His current projects include the expansion of The Inspiration Book Series™ & The What College Forgets To Teach You® Multimedia Transformation System. In addition, Anthony provides one-to-one coaching services to highly motivated & committed professionals and student leaders.

FOR MORE INFORMATION CALL: 1.877.338.8246
OR VISIT US ONLINE ATWWW.COLLEGIATE-EMPOWERMENT.COM

Order Books Direct & Save Money!

Inspiration Books make great gifts for your students & members. Are you looking for a great way to say thank you, congratulations, welcome or job well done?

# of Books	Approx. Discount	Per Copy	Bulk Rate Discount	You Save	S&H	Total Price
1-9	NA	$14.95	NA	NA	$1.50 ea.	$16.45
10	10%	$13.45	$134.50	$15.00	$8	$142.50
25	15%	$12.70	$317.50	$56.25	$10	$327.50
50	20%	$12.00	$600.00	$147.50	$20	$620.00
75	25%	$11.25	$843.75	$277.50	$25	$868.75
100	30%	$10.50	$1050.00	$445.00	$40	$1090.00
150	35%	$9.75	$1462.50	$780.00	$50	$1512.50
200	40%	$9.00	$1800.00	$1190.00	$60	$1860.00

We accept checks, purchase orders & major credit cards.

To Place Your Order Contact
The Collegiate EmPowerment Company, Inc.
Call Toll Free: 1.877.EDUTAIN (338.8246)
Fax Your Order To: 609.397.0833
Or Email Your Order To:
Inspiration@Collegiate-EmPowerment.com